The Ethics of Territorial Borders

Also by John Williams

THE ANARCHICAL SOCIETY IN A GLOBALIZED WORLD (*co-editor with Richard Little*)

GLOBAL CITIZENSHIP: A Critical Reader (*co-editor with Nigel Dower*)

HANNAH ARENDT AND INTERNATIONAL RELATIONS: Readings across the Lines (*co-editor with Anthony F. Lang, Jr*)

LEGITIMACY IN INTERNATIONAL RELATIONS AND THE RISE AND FALL OF YUGOSLAVIA

The Ethics of Territorial Borders

Drawing Lines in the Shifting Sand

John Williams

Lecturer in International Relations
University of Durham, UK

First published 2006 by
PALGRAVE MACMILLAN
Houndmills, Basingstoke, Hampshire RG21 6XS and
175 Fifth Avenue, New York, N.Y. 10010
Companies and representatives throughout the world

PALGRAVE MACMILLAN is the global academic imprint of the Palgrave
Macmillan division of St. Martin's Press, LLC and of Palgrave Macmillan Ltd.
Macmillan® is a registered trademark in the United States, United Kingdom
and other countries. Palgrave is a registered trademark in the European
Union and other countries.

ISBN-13: 978–0–230–00252–4 hardback
ISBN-10: 0–230–00252–8 hardback

This book is printed on paper suitable for recycling and made from fully
managed and sustained forest sources.

A catalogue record for this book is available from the British Library.

Library of Congress Cataloging-in-Publication Data
Williams, John, 1969–
    The ethics of territorial borders : drawing lines in the shifting sand / John
Williams.
        p.   cm.
    Includes bibliographical references and index.
    ISBN 0–230–00252–8
    1. Boundaries—Moral and ethical aspects.   2. Political geography—
Moral and ethical aspects.   3. International relations—Moral and
ethical aspects.   I. Title.
JC323.W55 2006
172'.4—dc22   2005056368

10   9   8   7   6   5   4   3   2   1
15   14   13   12   11   10   09   08   07   06

Printed and bound in Great Britain by
Antony Rowe Ltd, Chippenham and Eastbourne

Again, for Susan

Contents

Acknowledgements

The origins of this book can be traced to a presentation I gave to the departmental research seminar in the Department of Politics and International Relations at Aberdeen University in the early spring of 1997. This was the first paper I had given to my new colleagues, having been appointed to my first academic job in the department a few months earlier. I forget what the paper was about, but one of the questions set in train the thought processes that have finally produced this book. Amongst the audience was Gordon Graham, Regius Professor of Moral Philosophy, who said that whilst he found the arguments I had made interesting, they could only be valid if I could explain to him why territorial borders had any moral standing. This was not a matter to which I had given any thought at all and after opening and closing my mouth in the manner of a gold-fish for what felt like a very long time, I offered an answer which even I knew to be inadequate. My first vote of thanks must therefore go to him for that question. I am only sorry that it has taken so long to offer a reasonably well-thought-through answer.

From that point onwards I have been thinking about the ethics of territorial borders, alongside other things and amidst the usual distractions and commitments of academic life. These thoughts have underpinned a small number of papers and articles on the subject, two of which provide the basis for two of the chapters in this book, although they appear here in substantially modified and expanded form. I therefore wish to acknowledge the permission of Frank Cass publishers to reuse material first published as 'Territorial Borders, International Ethics and Political Geography: Do Good Fences Still Make Good Neighbours?' in *Geopolitics*, Volume 8, Number 2, 2003, in Chapter 2 of this book. I would also like to acknowledge the permission of Cambridge University Press to reuse material first published as 'Territorial Borders, Toleration and the English School' in *Review of International Studies*, Volume 28, Number 4, 2002, in Chapter 4.

The process of writing those papers and presenting earlier versions of them and others to conferences and seminars has brought me into contact with a number of people whose work has inspired and influenced me and who, perhaps even more importantly, have been willing to discuss these and other questions with me and offer encouragement as I have tried to work things out in my own mind. Many of these people are to be found in the references and bibliography that follow, but I wish to single out, in no particular order, Chris Brown, Nick Rengger, Nigel Dower, Barry Buzan, Richard Little and Andrew Linklater for particular mention in this regard. The undergraduate students who have taken my course 'the ethics of violence in international relations' over the years may also recognise a good deal of what follows and may now see themselves as having been unwitting, but very helpful, guinea pigs in the testing of ideas and arguments.

The main period of writing this book was thankfully covered by a period of research leave, helping to minimise its impact on family life. Nevertheless, my wife, Susan, and children, Eleanor and Thomas, have had to put up with some fairly distracted behaviour as ideas stumbled into dead ends, drafts were discarded, writer's block encountered and the other setbacks this kind of exercise produces were endured. They deserve great credit for putting up with me and even professing that most of the time they like me and have been glad to have had me around the house during the writing of this book.

John Williams
Durham, September 2005

1
Introduction

Lines in the shifting sands

The line in the sand is a familiar allusion, even if only from the legend of The Alamo. The image of a leader dragging a stick, or, perhaps better still, a bayonet, through the dust to mark the point beyond which an enemy will not be allowed to advance has powerful resonance in political life well beyond popular culture. It is a declaration of ownership; a way of marking what is ours from what is theirs; a statement of intent to defend that claim to possession; and a deliberate and wilful act. The line in the sand therefore possesses many of the characteristics that we tend to associate with territorial borders in international politics. The lines on the map, some of which are indeed through the sand of the world's deserts and arid areas, are popularly thought of as possessing these same kinds of characteristics, and with similar military undertones.

This idea is a very powerful one, so powerful, in fact, that it is often taken for granted. In such a view, territorial borders must be about delimiting ownership, about delimiting authority, about establishing defensive lines and marking the difference between 'us' and 'them'. Such functions may even be assumed to be natural, linked to the physical geographical features of rivers, deserts, seas and ridges of mountain ranges that often provide the topographical location of territorial borders. These ideas and claims, though, have come under growing pressure, to the point where the sands have shifted far enough that the symbolism of the line in the sand, or on the map, is arguably losing its resonance.[1] These challenges take a great many

1

forms, more than any single volume could attempt to discuss systematically and in detail. Thus this introduction offers some brief discussion of what the book is not about, setting in context the more detailed discussions to follow.

Borders and globalisation

Most dramatic are the claims of the creation of a 'borderless world', probably most closely associated with the work of Kenichi Ohmae, and the idea that globalisation, and especially the transfer of power away from states towards corporations, is resulting in a global economic system that increasingly operates in ways that make the idea of a territorial border largely meaningless.[2] This is creating new types of social, political and economic space that by their very nature cannot be bordered in a way that is comparable to the ways in which we create borders between states at present. Ideas such as 'supra-territoriality' refer to spaces that exist beyond the limitations of physical space – that have no location in terms of longitude, latitude and altitude.[3] The cyberspace of the Internet is one such example, the global financial system another.

The creation of these new social, political and economic spaces is leading to the creation of new forms of social, political and economic actors. The idea of 'global citizenship' throws up a nice example of two different, and competing, interpretations of the possibilities for new types of politics in new types of spaces.[4] On the one hand comes the idea of individuals who think of themselves as being 'citizens of the world' or 'cosmopolites' to borrow the phrase associated with the Stoics of the classical world who are so often seen as being the originators of global citizenship.[5] In contemporary terms, such global citizens are seen as possessing a political and ethical vision that is global in its extent and concerns. This means not necessarily and automatically privileging the needs, interests or desires of a geographically specific and bordered group of people with whom one shares membership of a state. It means recognising and accepting the moral standing of all human beings, or, potentially, all living things, and that their sharing or not sharing membership of a state is morally arbitrary. Political loyalty to a state is also morally arbitrary, and thus non-binding. It is the right, and perhaps even the duty, of the global citizen to challenge those who govern the place where they happen to live should that government act in ways that reject the moral equality of all in the name of furthering the narrow interests of the few.[6]

A second way of thinking about global citizenship, though, is found in the corporate world, where corporations declare themselves to be 'global citizens' or identify their highest flying (often, it seems, literally given the propensity for business-class travel) executives as 'global citizens'. Whilst sharing to some extent the idea of citizenship as bringing responsibilities that is characteristic of the first version of global citizenship, these corporate actors are usually keener to stress the idea of citizenship bringing with it rights, and particularly the rights to exploit global markets, global access and global opportunities in pursuit of the generation of wealth. This, the claim runs, brings with it benefits for all in terms of economic growth, offering a chance for all to become more prosperous, with something of a veil drawn over the widening inequalities in how wealth is distributed. Instead, the real challenge facing the global citizens is the welter of restrictions, tariffs, taxes, quotas and so on placed in the way of those looking to do business. The global outlook is not so much the idea of a universal or cosmopolitan moral framework, but the commonalities of business. Capitalism as a border-busting activity brings with it a whole host of costs and benefits that are not the concern of this book, but it reinforces the idea that economic activity is playing an important role in challenging the idea of territorial borders.[7]

Notions of an emerging global civil society and of transnational social movements further add to claims about the inability of a strictly territorially bordered conception of politics to encompass adequately the range of important non-state social, political and economic actors at play in the international, or perhaps global, political world.[8] Networks, whether formal such as those environmental groups affiliated to Greenpeace, for example, or more informal, such as the remarkably disparate collection of activists who coordinate their protests against globalisation at meetings like the World Economic Forum or the G-8, have become crucial to these political forms.[9] Formal, institutionalised and hierarchical structures plugged into the political institutions of a single state are being replaced by looser, less state-based and more flexible structures, focused on specific issues, like the environment, third world debt, human rights and women's issues, or to specific events, like the 2003 Iraq War or major UN conferences on the environment.[10]

The shifting of the sands is thus conceived of as taking place in a number of different domains and at different levels of international politics, resulting in actors operating on a multi-dimensional playing field, to shift the metaphor temporarily. The category of 'global' is thus commonly added to the levels of local, national and international politics and the idea of new places, spaces, conditions, actors and processes that come with the new level are widely debated.[11] This debate, of course, considers far more than the fate of territorial borders, but it does provide an important context for the more specific question of territorial borders and the even more specific one of the ethics of those borders.

By calling into question their importance in the way the world works, or does not work, depending on your perspective, these developments implicitly raise the issue of whether we should welcome or fear these developments.[12] The chances are, of course, that given the scale and complexity of the issues that have arisen we are more likely to welcome some aspects of these changes and deplore others, whilst perhaps also feeling that some are beyond our control or have, at least, now got beyond our control. For example, it does not seem far-fetched to imagine an individual who welcomes challenges to the presumption of non-intervention in the domestic affairs of a sovereign state in the face of major human rights abuses, but is just as concerned at the loss of a government's ability to control labour standards or to have the final say on whether a proposed foreign direct investment should be allowed to go ahead or not. Equally, she may feel that the world's financial markets are now essentially beyond the control of political authority, due to the massive scale of transactions, and we must just keep our fingers crossed and hope that the system does not suffer a catastrophic failure.

Where we retain control, at some level or other, the question arises of the basis upon which we should make judgements about what to do and whether that basis should be coherent and consistent, as opposed to an *ad hoc* approach that treats each issue or problem as it arises. There is, or at least so this book wishes to contend, an important ethical dimension to this discussion that cannot be avoided, or separated out: such issues are inherently and unavoidably ethical.

Changing interstate relations and territorial borders

So far, this summary has stressed the challenges to the status of territorial borders that have arisen from globalisation, in its various guises. However, there are, of course, also a great many political developments coming from within states, and arising in the 'classical' domain of interstate relations – foreign policy, military security and geo-politics. The end of the Cold War presented many such challenges, with the collapse of communism in eastern Europe bringing major changes to what had previously been presumed to be a settled map and that was suddenly thrown into doubt. How to respond to the demands for independence by the former Soviet Socialist Republics, by the members of the Socialist Federal Republic of Yugoslavia and by the desire of Czechoslovakia to break in two posed practical and intellectual challenges, especially where the result was the most extreme violence seen in Europe since the end of the Second World War, most notably in Bosnia. The location of the borders of new and successor states became vital political questions, and some novel solutions to seemingly intractable political problems were developed, such as the wonderfully ambiguously named 'inter-entity dividing line' between the two constituent parts of Bosnia Herzegovina.[13]

These claims, ideas and events, though, are usually importantly empirical. They rest on claims about the ways in which things are changing or have changed and about how social, political and economic dynamics are forcing us to re-think the significance of the lines on the map and where they are to be drawn. The sands are in some cases shifting almost physically, as the disputed border between Eritrea and Ethiopia across the Ogaden desert most literally attests. Debates about the extent of these changes are ongoing, too, with the extent and significance of globalisation being hotly debated.[14] However, for the purposes of this book, the empirical aspects of the debate about the decline, or transformation, or irrelevance of territorial borders is of secondary concern. Equally, arguments about the physical location of territorial borders between 'new' states are not the principal subject matter here. These issues arise, as they unavoidably must in any work looking at territorial borders, but they are used in a way that is illustrative of different sorts of questions and challenges. The argument here is that a focus on the empirical can continue to repeat what I want to argue are limitations in dominant or mainstream thinking about territorial borders because it causes us to overlook the significance of different kinds of border questions – to fail to fully appreciate the significance of shiftings that have and are continuing to take place in different sorts of sands.

These challenges are theoretical and conceptual ones. They are more purely intellectual, the result of the growing engagement of international relations and political geography with post-positivist intellectual trends and the growing concern, most notable in international relations, with re-thinking the methodology of the discipline. Most importantly, these trends present us with different sorts of questions about borders than those arising from the dissolution of states or the ongoing processes of globalisation. In particular, they cast into doubt the ontological status of territorial borders, questioning in fundamental ways the idea of borders as 'material' or 'natural' or 'inevitable' and fixed in their meaning and role in politics.[15]

Instead, there is a great emphasis on treating borders as a social practice. By this I mean the idea that what a border is, what it means and what it does are not separable from what human beings think about these questions and that a complex relationship between ideas and social action based on ideas underpins the construct of 'territorial border'.[16] It may be the case, and this has become a commonplace in critical discussions of borders, that a great many human beings have thought the same thing about these questions, even to the extent that we have tended to stop thinking about them, so obvious, or settled, or commonsensical seem the answers.[17] Territorial borders have thus suffered the fate of reification, and this has tended to either stunt or divert discussions about their role in international politics. The kinds of empirically focused approaches to borders roughed out above have tended to concentrate on the border by-passing or negating aspects of activity, working on the assumption that territorial borders are one type of thing and that they are unable to change or take on different forms. Equally, the possibility of a new form of bordering emerging from these developments tends to be underplayed because they do not create the kind of social practices we tend to assume are emblematic of territorial borders – the division of zones of authority and ownership symbolised by claims to sovereignty.

Returning borders to the social world, though, opens a host of possibilities for renewed investigation. Some of these link clearly to the kind of empirical challenges discussed above – asking questions like: what kinds of social practices are most important in challenging the established roles and functions of territorial borders; what are the mechanisms by which social practices prove successful in challenging borders; how do new social practices spread through the international political system; can we model and consequently predict the kinds of social practices that are likely to succeed in changing patterns of behaviour and thinking, and those which will not?[18] These are the kinds of questions that explore the relationship between social action and the conduct of international politics as it is usually studied, bringing with them the potential to connect the social sciences' long-standing preference for empirical research and a deep-rooted philosophical realism to more ideational and social phenomena.[19]

The potential for such work is one that has considerable appeal, perhaps particularly in the United States where the privileging of positivist social science methodologies in international relations has long been strongest.[20] The desire is evident to give social constructivism a 'proper' research programme and a series of studies that will enable identification, perhaps even quantification, of ideational and other social phenomena in a pattern of independent and dependent variables.[21] Looking beyond international relations to the realm of political geography, such a methodological move is appealing because of the strength of the case-study as a research method to be found there. Indeed, one of the striking things, to those from an international relations background, about political geography is the dominance of the case-study method as the principal mechanism for exploring geographical phenomena.

However, this effort to build a bridge across the purported divide between positivist and post-positivist methodologies comes at a not inconsiderable price, one that this study is unwilling to pay, given its desire to address the ethical and normative aspects of territorial borders. A post-positivist methodological approach is necessary, the book argues, to get to grips with the ethical issues and questions that have tended to be overlooked. This is because of the way that it restores a major role for ideas and the social practices that ideas help to define and shape. It thus restores the role of choice to international politics in a way that not only goes beyond some rather deterministic approaches to international relations where reified and largely immutable social structures push human agents around,[22] but also by offering a concept of choice that goes further than policy options. This requires us to recognise deficiencies in the way that ethics have often been discussed in international relations, too.

Ethics and 'International Political Theory'[23]

International ethics has often been discussed in the past in terms of which policy option is the more 'ethical', based on an assumption that ethics are in some important sense separate from the policy world, providing a check-list or yard-stick against which policy decisions can be measured. A useful illustration of this is the portrayal of Just War thinking in such a fashion, with the classic criteria of the *jus ad bellum* and the *jus in bello* being held up as the very essence of what it means to use military force in an ethical manner, with any departure from the criteria resulting in serious doubt being cast on the justice of a conflict or of its conduct.[24] The conclusion to be drawn from such failings is that here is evidence of the amorality, if not immorality, of an international political world where the national interest and *realpolitik* are to be found behind all political actions. The question, 'What are their real motives?' is almost always heard, for example, when political leaders claim to be acting on the basis of ethical ideas, reflecting an assumption that such talk can be only that – talk.

The idea remains popular of there being two worlds – one of politics and one of ethics – with only good fortune, or very low opportunity costs, causing a genuine, as opposed to rhetorical, overlap between them in policy-making. A deep-rooted methodological suspicion of ethics as 'opinion' lacking proper, demonstrable causes and effects has reinforced this sidelining in the academic world of international relations. We cannot properly 'know' what effect an ethical idea has on political action because measuring intentions is extremely difficult and it is almost impossible to compare the effect of such ethical 'opinions' and 'ideas' on the decisions made by different actors. Treating ideational and social elements of international politics in a way that fits with positivist ideas of what 'proper' research programmes ought to be tends to repeat this pattern, and produces the same unsatisfactory results.[25]

Ethics, this book suggests, following many others, are not about a bolt-on choice to be made, judged against externally produced reference points that exist separate from the political process, and rooted in an essentially different world to that of political choices and decisions.[26] Treating them in this way has a number of theoretical problems attached to it, some of them with a long and venerable history in Western thinking about politics and ethics. As Kimberley Hutchings has demonstrated this can be traced back to St Augustine, with the division continuing, and in her view continuing to be unhelpful, into contemporary efforts to think about ethics and politics, and especially international politics where moral scepticism has been particularly strong.[27] Whilst not following Hutchings through to her final conclusions about what overcoming this separation means for ethical thought in international relations, this book does want to support the claim that the idea of ethical choices being different to and separate from political choices is mistaken.

In particular, the idea that political structures are importantly, if not almost entirely, ideational, rather than material, and thus the product of human agency massively extends the realm and role of choice in international politics, and with choice comes ethics.[28] If the nature, meaning and role of, for example, territorial borders are not determined by some material structure, but are instead the result of a long series of human choices and decisions, then it is both reasonable and necessary to examine the thinking that saw some choices taken over others and to insist on the possibility of changing the way of thinking in the present and future with a view to addressing injustices, inequities and other ethical problems with currently dominant ideas. The only way out of this is to make the rather implausible claim that we live in the best of all possible worlds and that we have thus attained some sort of ethical perfection. Making such a claim in the face of famine, genocide, terrorism, absolute poverty and so on would be heroic enough, adding in the diversity of ideas about what ethical perfection would look like emphasises the fantastical nature of any such claim. There is a real need for ethical thinking in international relations and for ethical attention to be focused on aspects of the international political system, like territorial borders, that have been taken for granted and treated as though they were material facts, and not social practices.

The structure of the book

Chapter 2 of the book looks at this methodological argument in more detail, engaging with these debates at some length in order to explore both how the idea of territorial borders has been reified in the past and what this means for efforts to re-think territorial borders in the present and in the future. Thus, we are not at the mercy of a deterministic, capitalist process of globalisation whereby borders will be shaped and changed in the future by impersonal and uncontrollable forces irrespective of what human beings want, and what they believe to be right. Neither do we face some kind of fixed choice between a borderless world and the retention of the current structures and understandings. One of the goals of the book is to show that borders are indeed being re-thought in contemporary politics, even in arenas like military security and the use of force where we might expect the established pattern to be at its most powerful and persuasive. This is not being driven by exogenous material forces, but by how political actors are responding to the kinds of problems and challenges that ask difficult questions of established understandings. The examples of 'humanitarian intervention' and the 'war on terror' are deployed here, and elsewhere in the book, to offer illustration, connecting the theoretical side of the book with the contemporary political context.

Chapter 2 shows that the connections between ideas about territorial borders and the social practices that have defined borders and that accumulate around them are part of a complex process. The chapter tries to simplify this, as all theoretical propositions do, but its main stress is on the way that borders are an importantly ideational practice, and one in which agency is prominent. We do have options, we can make choices about how we understand the role and nature of territorial borders in international politics and these choices are significantly ethical ones. This is not just in the 'yardstick' sense of whether or not choices conform to established frameworks of ethical thinking, but also about how they unavoidably contain ethical aspects, through the choices that are made about which routes to take, which problems to prioritise, which arguments and evidence to deploy, which language is used. The characterisation of the 'war on terror' and the way in which leading politicians in the United Kingdom and the United States discussed the justification of military action against Iraq also help to show that this is a contested process – even between two close allies the intellectual framing of post-9/11 territorial borders is a topic of debate, often unconsciously. As we shall see in Chapter 2, this is not to suggest that there is an ethical free-for-all in the sense that we can simply re-think territorial borders in accordance with some overarching ethical agenda or blueprint for a better world. The legacy of our dominant understanding of territorial borders, as with so many other structures, is a powerful one. But it is not immutable and the book moves on in Chapter 3 to look at some of the opportunities and problems that arise in re-thinking territorial borders. In particular, the chapter looks at the idea of territorial borders possessing ethical value. This itself raises two questions: is this value inherent in the idea of territorial borders; or is ethical significance derivative from the ability of borders to contribute to the attainment of something that is ethically valued? The argument here is that in most discussions of territorial borders it is the latter – the ethical significance that they possess is not because there is something ethical about the idea of territorial borders, but that the institution of territorial borders, as usually understood in international relations, serves useful functions in attaining, or at least contributing to the partial attainment of, an ethically desirable outcome.

The argument here focuses on the idea of order and the claims, most commonly associated with the English school of international relations theory, that the system of sovereign states, in which territorial borders play a fundamental role, is potentially ethically defensible because it enables a degree of orderliness to exist in relations between states. In particular, without this order-generating system, the world would face a situation in which power, particularly military power, would be unbridled and war and violence would become ubiquitous, with a concomitant decline in the possibility of trust that underpins, among many other things, international trade, diplomacy, international law and the workings of almost all important international social, political and economic organisations. The idea of territorial borders as the boundaries between sovereign states has enabled a rich skein of rules to develop about the ownership of property and the ways in which it can be transferred, about when it is permissible to resort to force and about who the actors are that are permitted to enter into international agreements and the kinds of subjects those agreements can cover. We tamper with this at our peril.[29]

The fragility, or otherwise, of this international society of states is debated within the English school, but rather than follow that argument through, the book wants to look at other ways of reinforcing the ethical status of territorial borders by moving the argument away from the idea of borders as possessing derivative ethical significance principally in relation to order.[30]

The tension between order and justice is one that is well known in the English school approach that provides the starting point for exploring the ethics of territorial borders in Chapter 3, whilst suggesting that this is an unnecessarily restrictive intellectual framework to deploy.[31] Instead, the chapter tries to draw on more expressly liberal ways of approaching the derivative significance of territorial borders, which it argues are inherent in the English school in any case. In particular, the idea of territorial borders being a necessary element of a system of rights is considered, drawing on the idea of rights and duties of special beneficence that may exist amongst individuals and between groups.

This provides the chapter with a way of looking at how many cosmopolitan approaches to normative theory in international relations, with their emphasis on universality, nevertheless require mechanisms for reflecting ethical particularism within the overarching confines of a universal schema. The chapter considers, again, how post-9/11 political debates have reflected this problem, with interesting consequences for the way in which territorial borders have been discussed in relation to Iraq before and since the 2003 war. This shows a sharp move away from the classical questions of geo-politics and a move towards an understanding of the role of territorial borders in relation to order and security in international politics that is far more focused on the character of the regime governing a territory than the location of territorial borders. This links to the issue of the management of diversity, with territorial borders being one way of doing this, but only one way, and the empirical challenges to the centrality of borders to thinking about citizenship, community and identity, for example, are arguably rendering this function less important. Nevertheless, it is one that is relatively under-explored in cosmopolitan literature and does throw up some interesting ideas about how a liberal, cosmopolitan international political theory may well require some form of territorial bordering as a part of its make-up.[32]

Nevertheless, this means that the ethical status of territorial borders remains overwhelmingly derivative. There does not, on the liberal reading offered in Chapter 3, seem to be good, ethical reasons why we should grant territorial borders ethical standing and attach to them certain ideas in and of themselves. There is no reason, other than the needs of the higher ethical goals of either order, or a liberal world, or some combination of the two, which would cause us to treat territorial borders as possessing ethical significance. The task of Chapter 4 is to outline an argument that territorial borders might, nevertheless, play such an intrinsically ethically valuable role. This is a tall order, as it requires an argument that sees territorial borders as part of an answer to the great ethical question of 'How might we live?' Offering an answer that, at least in part, includes the words, 'In a world divided by territorial borders', is unlikely to leap to anyone's mind, at least in contrast with phrases such as, 'In a just world' or 'In a peaceful world'.[33]

Chapter 4, though, argues that the issue of ethical diversity matters here and that territorial borders are a vital part of a normative vision that values the ethical diversity of the world, seeing it as a positive thing that people should preserve, protect and treasure. In particular, ethical diversity – both the fact of it and the value that it should be seen to possess – requires a global ethic of toleration.

Toleration, it should be noted, is often seen as a distinctively liberal ethic, traceable back to John Locke in particular, but Chapter 4 points to problems with the liberal approach to toleration that render it unsuitable to circumstances of profound ethical disagreement, such as those that characterise international politics.[34] This is not to deny the force of the liberal argument, which is very significant and informs a good deal of the political debate about how different societies, cultures or civilisations can rub along together in the world, or not, as the case may be. It is, though, to suggest that a liberal approach to toleration struggles to deal with the extent of ethical diversity in the world because it fails to truly value the difference it claims to accommodate.

Specifically, the chapter deploys an argument more indebted to the civic republican tradition, and specifically indebted to the political thought of Hannah Arendt, to make an argument about the ethical necessity of difference and the need for divisions between the different, including territorial divisions. This is not to make some kind of case for essential and fixed division on the grounds of nationality, race, religion, culture, or some other form of relativistic argument. Instead it is to see separation as part of a global ethic of toleration and that this separation needs to take a territorial form, or, more weakly, that it always has taken a territorial form and that there are no compelling reasons to believe that it will not continue to do so.

It is important, even at this early stage, to reiterate that this is not an argument for fixing the present lines on the map, whether through sand or otherwise, for ever. The present location of the lines is, indeed, ethically arbitrary in the sense that the role that borders play is potentially separable from their location. This may often be, though, a principally theoretical point – a claim about the logic of the argument in favour of the ethical significance inherent in territorial borders. The specific value of particular territorial borders as they exist in the world is often linked to physical place, with nationalism having played a hugely important role in attaching certain communities to pieces of land that become 'homelands'.[35] This, of course, creates enormous practical political difficulties over the location of territorial borders in places such as Palestine and Kosovo where the idea of 'holy land' comes into play.[36] As such, Chapter 4 will attempt to address these questions. It does not offer a 'solution' to where to draw the lines on the map in these instances, but it does try to detach the particular problems that arise and are attached to the border in cases such as these from the idea of territorial borders *per se* possessing ethical significance.

The book concludes, in Chapter 5, by returning to where we have started, by offering a more wide-ranging assessment of what this discussion of the ethics of territorial borders means for the study of territorial borders in wider terms. In particular, the argument about the focus of studies of borders is returned to, emphasising the benefits, and, indeed, necessity, of recognising the ethical dimension of territorial borders and thus the need for normative theorising about them. It is here that there is a more explicit appeal for the bringing closer together of international relations theory with political geography. In international relations, normative questions have, if not moved centre-stage, at least regained a position of importance and respectability after a long period during the Cold War when such matters were badly neglected. However, whilst there have been some appeals for a normative or ethical 'turn' in political geography, these have not been heard to any great extent in the discussion of borders.[37] Thus the seriousness with which the idea of the line in the sand or on the map has been treated by political geographers has not been fully picked up on international relations, particularly by international political theorists who have tended to assume that borders have only contingent ethical significance. Conversely, political geographers have not recognised the power of the ethical and normative critique being mounted within international relations and the relevance of this to the study of borders.

It is, therefore, time to turn to the question of what territorial borders are and how we do, can and should think about them if we are to recognise and engage with their ethical significance. This discussion is, necessarily, a methodological one that turns on some technical distinctions. However, we shall also see how, consciously or not, some of the opportunities for change that are opened by a recognition of the inadequacies of a strongly materialist notion of borders are being utilised by the political leaders of the United States and the United Kingdom in recent years to address the political agenda of the war on terror and their take on the challenges of globalisation.

2
From Material Facts to Social Practices

Introduction

The division of the world into what John Gerard Ruggie calls 'distinct, disjoint and mutually exclusive territorial formations' lies at the heart of an international politics based upon the relations between sovereign states.[1] Some of our most basic or foundational constitutive ideas about international relations, like sovereignty, are inextricably linked to specifiable pieces of territory. This, by definition, requires territorial borders that serve as the dividing lines between political entities. This division has come to take a specific form through the development of sovereignty – the idea of 'the razor's edge', associated with Lord Curzon, nicely illustrates the notion of a precise, fine and yet hard divide – with ownership and authority being both absolute and completely distinct on either side.[2]

Sovereignty as a concept has been the subject of something of a re-birth in interest in recent years, with a series of studies looking at the origins and development of the institution and the ways in which its contemporary manifestations in practice inevitably depart from conceptual purity. Stephen Krasner's description of sovereignty as 'organized hypocrisy' is perhaps the most striking, but we have become used to seeing sovereignty assaulted.[3]

However, the sovereignty critique does not extend terribly far into looking at the territorial borders that specify the extent of sovereign authority. There appears to be an assumption that the status of territorial borders and the role that they play is inextricable from the larger picture of the fate of sovereignty. If sovereignty declines in

16

importance or changes in its nature then territorial borders will change too in order to accommodate the needs for a 'new' sovereignty regime or some alternative 'primary', 'foundational' or 'bedrock' institution, to borrow terms from Barry Buzan.[4] This certainly shows a welcome recognition of the dynamism of sovereignty as a concept, reflecting a waking up in international relations to the historical fact that sovereignty was not born, fully-fledged, at the Peace of Westphalia in 1648 but has, instead, undergone a whole series of developments, changes and re-definitions since the middle of the seventeenth century, if not well before then, with some tracing the origins of the modern concept of sovereignty back to the twelfth century.[5]

However, and here is the challenge for this chapter, this leaves territorial borders under-theorised. They become a slave to the master of sovereignty, a feature of international politics whose role is wholly dependent on the fate of sovereignty. Should we move into a 'post-Westphalian' or 'neo-medieval' age then we can expect that territorial borders will stop playing the role of delimiting zones of claims to exclusive sovereignty and start playing some sort of other role.[6] As with the idea of 'neo-medievalism', history may give us some clues as to what to expect.

Past experience of frontier-zones are one possible guide – strips of territory of variable width and location where the authority of one metropolitan centre phases out, whilst the authority of another phases in. This may leave the people of such areas enjoying the opportunities of playing one power centre off against another to create valuable commercial opportunities for activities that can exist in the nether world between the rules. It may create new, self-conscious 'border-lander' identities, people who see themselves as defined by their position between others, being neither one thing nor another, but different because of their dual enculturation or because of their notion of themselves as 'frontierspeople' – those operating at the margins of a civilisation. The fate of such people may, though, be a perpetual frontline – occupying a zone where instability, violence and conflict are perennial as different metropolitan powers try to assert their authority or, more sinister, agree that a particular place will be the agreed location of their struggle in order to contain it.[7]

These more anthropological speculations may indeed have historical parallels – it does not take a lot of imagination to fit the people of the medieval Welsh marches, of the nineteenth-century American

West, of the early modern Balkans and Baltic and of the northwest of the British Raj into the kinds of categories roughed out above. However, the future is not the past and whilst such parallels are useful heuristic devices for pointing to the need for diversity of thinking, they are unlikely to prove terribly accurate predictors of what a 'post-Westphalian' age is to look like. However, they do point towards the idea of territorial borders as being social practices that can exist independently of sovereignty. Human beings have had a need to think about and construct their understanding of the land (and sea, too, but that is very much a secondary concern in this book) upon which they live in social, political and economic conditions that are not characterised by the presence of Westphalian understandings of sovereignty.

This recognition of the possibility of differently territorially bordered political, social and economic entities also raises the possibility, of course, of borderless social forms.[8] Whilst the more zealous advocates of globalisation may see trends in the global economy and in the potential of technological transformation that will eclipse established and historical notions of borders, the durability of bordering behaviour and the entrenchment in the present political situation of the sovereign state would seem to suggest that territorial borders will be around for some time to come as an important feature of our principal political formations. One of the arguments that this book is aiming to make, of course, is that we also *should* see territorial borders as such a feature, that there is a normative case to be made on the basis of the ethical value that can inhere in territorial borders that makes them a desirable feature of any political disposition.

Making this case, though, requires us to accept the portrayal of territorial borders as social practices and as such the product of human agency and choice, as it is with agency that we get ethics. This requires a rejection of the idea that territorial borders are either exclusively or, for the argument here, even predominantly 'natural' in the sense that they occur irrespective of any human agency. The idea of a state possessing 'natural' borders is therefore rejected. This is not to deny, of course, that features of the natural world may serve the function of a border – there are all sorts of reasons (and not all of them military) why rivers, seas, mountain ridges and deserts should serve as the location of a territorial border. However, that is a very long way from saying that they *must* serve as territorial borders; that there is something in and of those physical geographical features that determines their social and political role as a territorial border, irrespective of anything human beings may choose to try and do about it.

Establishing this kind of argument has been an important trend in political geography, and especially in what has come to be known as 'critical geopolitics' over the last 10 years or so.[9] As suggested above, whilst international relations has been slow to address the issue of territorial borders *per se*, preferring instead to leave them tied up with sovereignty, it too has undergone a major methodological debate during the last 15 years that has been conducive to seeing such features as social practices. In particular, the normative questions that are opened once we start to adopt such a position have been a particular feature of the way that international relations has responded to these methodological moves. There have been a series of major and important works on normative theory in international relations,[10] and leading methodological statements about what is often known as 'post-positivism' recognise the normative potential within their arguments and the relevance of such issues, even where they do not devote themselves to them.[11]

This position is somewhat in contrast to political geography, where the normative turn is one that is sometimes advocated, but more rarely taken.[12] This, though, presents this chapter with an opportunity to try and bring together the focus on re-conceptualising territorial borders that comes with the post-positivism of critical political geography and geopolitics with the engagement with ethical and normative issues that have been important in international relations.

Critical political geography meets international political theory

The rest of the chapter starts by looking briefly at how international relations has tended to think about territorial borders, and some of the reasons for this, and the costs involved. The emphasis is on borders as, basically, material phenomena that create certain sorts of political problems and related policy questions about how to deal with them. From here we move on to summarise the political geographic and international relations literatures that support the rest of the argument about the inadequacies of this approach.

We look at how political geography has challenged the reified image of territorial borders as 'fences' between sovereign spaces, and then considers the way in which boundaries and borders have been critiqued as part of the resurgence of international political theory, which has helped to propel ethical and normative issues more into the mainstream of international relations. The political geography literature receives slightly less attention. In part this reflects my background in international relations, but also because for my purposes the task is to establish the plausibility of territorial borders as social practices, rather than material facts, and thus amenable to ethical enquiry. Thus the richness of this literature in working through the geographical, social and political implications of challenged and differentiated borders is not fully reflected.

From here, we focus on a common question coming out of both approaches – the ontology of borders and subsequent methodological issues about how best to think about territorial borders. The chapter argues that despite our critique of a reified and static concept of borders, there is a need to recognise the strength of the border-as-fence analogy that plays such a fundamental role in the Westphalian notion of sovereignty. In particular, the paper critiques an ontologically minimalist approach to borders, often associated with post-modern or post-structural theory in international relations. This is not to deny the merits of such an approach *in toto*, but arguing instead that a 'neo-classical constructivism' offers a more appropriate methodology in considering both the ethical role territorial borders play and the role they ought to play in international relations.[13]

As stated, conventional IR theory sees territorial borders as being basically material features – part of the fixtures and fittings of the international system. They are contentious and controversial in their location, but not in the role they play. Disputes about territorial borders focus on where they are to be drawn, producing some of the most bitter and intractable political conflicts in international relations.[14] Ways of containing, if not resolving, these disputes have a chequered history.

Some have been 'solved' by force of arms – the so-called 'give war a chance' solution – whereby a state has been able to make its territorial claims stick in the face of all-comers for long enough that the status quo has come to be generally accepted, at least by those with power enough to do much about it by way of forcibly re-opening the dispute. Separatist and/or irredentist claims may persist, and may even produce violence, but not at a high enough level to persuade the sovereign power to relinquish control.

Many of the world's current territorial borders, especially in those parts of the world colonised by Europeans, have acquired their borders through imperial fiat. The colonial powers, most famously at meetings such as the Berlin West Africa Conference in 1884–5, negotiated the borders of their imperial possessions and drew the lines to suit their needs, and reflect their power, at that time. This was done with little or no regard for the interests, communities or developmental requirements of those they were dividing.

Seemingly more enlightened approaches to settling the location of borders may have been less bloody, at least in the short run, but do not guarantee automatically superior outcomes. Asking the people which state they would like to be a member of via plebiscites was discredited by the uses to which such votes were put by the Nazis. International judicial mechanisms have also been deployed, with legal rulings being issued. These, too, are far from universally accepted, with the party to the dispute whose case has been rejected able to reject the ruling in turn and return the dispute to the political, or even military, realm.

Perhaps the most common solution has been to simply put up with the situation, generally in the name of getting on with other things and avoiding the perils of re-opening old disputes or igniting new ones. The legal notion of the territorial integrity of states has within it a healthy measure of political pragmatism. A prime example is the agreement by the founders of the Organisation for African Unity in 1961 that the territorial borders of the growing number of sovereign states in Africa were arbitrary and absurd but also sacrosanct and immovable. Fear of the consequences of moving one and ending up fighting over them all was at root the cause of this decision. The 'lock-in' effect of the Westphalian notion of territorial borders, to borrow Chris Brown's phrase, should not be underestimated: the endurance of this conceptualisation is partially, but only partially, explained by the immense costs of changing it.[15]

All of these 'solutions' to the problem of where to draw the lines on the map share the conception of the delimitation of distinct, sovereign space as being the role of territorial borders. Challenges to this are, almost, unimaginable. To remove, or even to reconceptualise, territorial borders would mean the end of international relations as we know it, requiring a shift in the conduct of politics on the planet that is currently highly improbable. Certainly, dominant theories of international relations, whether neo-realism or liberal institutionalism, could not function without a reified notion of territorial borders. In the case of neo-realism in particular, the assumed political conse-quences that flow from such a territorial division – the unequal distribution of resources, the absence of over-arching political authority and the consequent chronic insecurity of states – practically defines what international relations can be about.[16] The famous dictum of Lord Curzon that 'Frontiers are indeed the razor's edge on which hang suspended the modern issues of war and peace, of life or death of nations' would seem to have been little challenged in inter-national relations theory, at least the mainstream of it, in the nearly hundred years since he made this comment.[17] The threat of 'life' or 'death' may have become less hyperbolic and more real with the development of nuclear weaponry, but this has served only to sharpen the question and focus minds, rather than to change the nature of the question itself.

David Newman and Anssi Paasi note that such a view held sway in geography until relatively recently, 'Geographers in particular seem to understand [territorial] boundaries as expressions or manifestations of the *territoriality of states* ... a spatial system which is characterised by more or less exclusive boundaries. This thinking shapes crucially the way in which we view the functioning and compartmentalization of the political organization of the world.'[18] Beyond this, it reinforces the idea coming from International Relations that the lines on the map are also the potential lines of conflict. This view can perhaps be summarised by one of the leading political geographers of borders, Gerald Blake, who portrayed borders as being a potential source of friction and even violence between states, should they fall into dispute. '[O]f fundamental importance is *political goodwill*. Unless neighbouring states have the political will to maintain good rela-tions, borderland harmony and cooperation will be impeded.'[19] Implicit in this is the idea that territorial borders are inherently a source of trouble that political leaders have to consciously attempt to overcome.

Thus the arguments of someone like Blake, that border issues are essentially a problem of policy and that territorial borders can be a forum for political hostility between states, stand as an example of the portrayal of territorial borders as static in role. His emphasis on the agreement, demarcation, maintenance and management of the border extends to the border's role in generating a sense of security for a state's citizens, linking easily with a traditional, state-centric and realist understanding of international relations.[20] Border issues are focused on the ability of the state to control what happens across borders, such as invasions, transnational crime and terrorism, refugee flows and pollution. For Blake, border disputes take place within this established and seemingly commonsensical understanding of the way the world is.[21] Borders are empirical facts.

In the Introduction, we looked briefly at some of the arguments for the border-busting nature of globalising capitalism, and the idea of the emergence of 'supra-territorial' spaces and the emergence of, again to borrow a neologism of Jan Aart Scholte's, the condition of 'globality'.[22] There are, of course, those who dispute the extent of globalisation, pointing to levels of trade interdependence little higher than those that existed amongst the European powers in the early 1910s, for example.[23] Others, such as Robert Jackson, argue that globalisation is highly unlikely to bring about any fundamental transformation in the nature of international politics because it cannot hope to create as successful a basis for the underpinning order as the existing international society.[24] Similarly, arguments for the extreme durability of established patterns come from different angles, with Colin Gray, for example, seeing no basis for believing that the pattern of international politics as being dominated by the age-old questions of war, peace and security will change. For him 'The future is the past – with GPS.'[25] The revolution that matters is not the creation of a globally framed economic space, with social and political aspects racing to catch up, but the revolution in military affairs that will transform the way in which conflict takes place.

The argument that 9/11 changed everything is another that Gray has no truck with, indeed, it is difficult to see him thinking that it changed anything very much at all.[26] However, the political responses to the attacks on the World Trade Center and Pentagon and the discussions of those responses that have taken place in the wider world are interesting for what they tell us about how we think about territorial borders. Here, I want to suggest, the more 'academic' methodological discussions that are the focus of our concern are being mirrored, if in a distorted way, by policy-makers and commentators.

These, I want to suggest, are showing tensions between pressures to adhere to a classic, Westphalian notion of territorial borders and the need to address a political and military adversary – transnational terrorism – that operates in ways that are not easily bordered in this sense. The former are evidenced by the way in which the immediate response to 9/11 was focused on Afghanistan – a sovereign state. Afghanistan, of course, had not attacked the United States directly, but the Bush Administration and the United Nations Security Council, which strongly backed US military action, placed a large proportion of the blame at the door of the Taliban government in Kabul because it had collaborated with and encouraged Al Qaeda by allowing it to set up training bases and use Afghanistan as a base for its leaders to plan operations. That the hijackers were predominantly Saudi Arabians and that planning and financing of the operation appear to have occurred in part in European states, including Germany, may be emblematic of the type of organisation Al Qaeda is (or was in 2001), but it made meshing a military response to its terrorism with the structure of international politics extremely difficult. Thus it was to the world's states that George W. Bush threw down the challenge to decide whether they were 'with us [the US], or with the terrorists.'[27]

This points to the difficulty in breaking out of the territorially bordered model of Westphalian politics. This is true even in the face of a challenge such as Al Qaeda that is so difficult to address because it does not conform to the Westphalian model in its structure, operation or political programme, in so much as it has one. Indeed, doubts about the existence of a meaningful, coherent or comprehensible political programme for such terrorism is linked to the way that such a programme bears only a passing resemblance to the territorialised version of politics that we take for granted. Aspects of Al Qaeda's programme may be territorially specific, such as the withdrawal of US and other Western forces from Saudi Arabia, or the destruction of the state of Israel, but the railing against 'decadence' and 'immorality' and 'infidels' and the ascription of enemy status on the basis of cultural or religious predilection is much harder to square with a territorially bordered politics. 'America' may be useful short-hand for Islamic fundamentalists, but it refers to so much more than the sovereign, territorially bordered USA.

This begins to point to connections to a critical approach to territorial borders described and developed by Newman and Paasi, who stress how it is that political geography has increasingly challenged the essentialised, reified view of territorial borders. In particular this comes through the use of techniques associated with post-modern and post-structural analyses of the social condition.[28] The idea of the border as delimiter of sovereignty is thus constructed and re-constructed in a search for control, linked to the nature of political, principally state, power and the idea of sovereignty. Reinforcing the borders in the face of threats is thus a way for the state to fulfil these kinds of expectations about what a state is, what it should do when in danger and how its power and control is concentrated above all within its territorial borders.

Jean Bethke Elshtain in her influential study of post-9/11 US politics argues strongly for the state as a territorially bordered entity in just this kind of way.[29] She points to the value of the state as being rooted in its ability to create a secure space for the population to enjoy the fruits of order, through the attainment of a vibrant civil society, and the creation of the kind of social, political, economic and judicial institutions that can enable higher goals, like culture, justice and democracy, to flourish. The creation and protection of what Elshtain calls 'ordinary civic peace'[30] is the principal purpose of the state and it is territorially bordered, creating a contrast with the war of all against all that is characteristic of the state of nature described by Hobbes and which Elshtain sees as lying in wait for those who fail to be vigilant in the protection of this civic peace. Because it is the state that creates this 'ordinary civic peace', Elshtain is compelled to join with the realist tradition in international relations in seeing the relations between states as lacking this civic character, as approaching the war of all against all that Hobbes famously describes. Where such civil society exists across or between states, it is because the states involved have themselves succeeded in creating a stable civic peace 'domestically'. This is the *sine qua non* of any sort of international or trans-national civil society.[31]

This is, though, to reify and essentialise borders in the way that we are seeking to challenge here. The idea that civility, perhaps even civilisation itself, is dependent on the territorial bordering of space into areas of sovereign control may be a feature of the Western tradition of political thought, but that does not exhaust by any means the ways of approaching such issues and questions. From an anthropological perspective, Hastings Donnan and Thomas Wilson join the critique of a reified borders-as-fences-between-states approach, '...these borders are constructed by much more than the institutions of the state which are present there, or of which the border's framework is a representative part.... Borders are also meaning-making and meaning-carrying entities, parts of the cultural landscape which often transcend the physical limits of the state and defy the power of state institutions.'[32] The attachment of 'ordinary civic peace' or other ethical categories and goods to territorial borders is a part of this meaning-making and meaning-carrying activity. It is not inherent in territorial borders, as a matter of material fact, that they have to play such roles or that they are essential to the creation of such values and circumstances. We may have come to understand them in this way, and Thomas Hobbes may have a big part to play in this, at least in the Western world, but this is the product of social practice and authoritative human intellectual investigation, rather than something over which people have no control. This is reinforced, and neatly summarised, by the claim that 'The border is not a spatial fact with a sociological impact, but a sociological fact that shapes spatially.'[33]

John Agnew and Stuart Corbridge have used a neo-Gramscian approach to describe the essentialised territorialisation of IR as 'the territorial trap' which has blinded analysts and theorists to the significance of the representation of territory in the development, maintenance and decline of hegemony.[34] Their argument is that borders have to be understood as being linked to the constellation of power that constitutes hegemony in such a way that not only does the hegemon exert potentially overwhelming force, but that such force acquires a degree of legitimacy and acceptance. The hegemon does not rely solely upon brute power, particularly violence, but is able to exert some degree of authority. The hegemon possesses a position of leadership that is, whether formally or not, socially sanctioned. Territorial borders are important here because they help to shape the sorts of ways that power is understood and help to de-legitimise challenges to established power that do not come through a state-like mechanism or entity. If only another state can challenge the leadership of the hegemonic power then other types of actors are at an automatic disadvantage both in terms of their ability to be politically effective, and also in their ability to attract public and scholarly attention.

We may therefore argue that part, but only part, of the reason for the dismissal of the political authenticity of a movement like Al Qaeda and the defence of the leading role of the state, and particularly of the United States, offered by someone like Elshtain is an acceptance of this 'territorial trap' and support for the hegemonic construction of territory. Clearly, not too much weight can be placed on this argument, with Elshtain's and other's denial of the validity of Al Qaeda and other Islamic fundamentalists stemming far more from moral abhorrence at their actions, goals and values.[35] However, that there is a 'race for the state' as the mechanism through which such fundamentalist ideas and actions should be defeated is instructive in the ways in which efforts to conceptualise post-9/11 politics have not sought to escape from the 'territorial trap'.

This reinforces the concern of politically astute anthropologists like Donnan and Wilson that borders are power structures. Borders are inextricably linked to the state's existence and this existence is linked to its ability, unique in the eyes of subscribers to the mainstream, to provide us with security. However, this existence is not as some sort of reified 'unit', existing in a system of 'like units' and subjected to the same structurally determined imperatives of action to defend those borders, as with neo-realism,[36] but as a nexus of power, identity, authority, legitimacy and other contested and contestable notions. Territorial borders are part of this contestation, their role, as opposed to their location, is in need of the same sort of critical examination to which other aspects of the state have been subjected.

Gearóid Ó Tuathail has applied Foucauldian and Derridean postmodernism to political geography to produce a coruscating critique of the uses of spatial representation for power-political purposes.[37] The nature of territorial borders as social and political constructs, intimately connected with the needs and purposes of dominant and hegemonic social groups and political constellations is therefore receiving serious attention. Tuathail provides perhaps the strongest appeal to us to reject the naturalisation of territorial division as being a part of the facts of geography; as natural as the rivers, deserts and mountain ranges that so often provide the physical inspiration for the cartographic precision of the lines on the map.[38]

As Newman notes, there is a need for what he calls a 'geography of boundary differentiation', that recognises the challenges, both theoretical and empirical, that the traditional account of territorial borders is facing, whilst retaining room for their enduring dividing roles.[39] We need a variety of ways of conceiving of borders and boundaries, noting that they serve multiple functions and are socially constructed in different ways. This is most true in relation to different times and different places, but there is a need to differentiate social practices tied up with a specific border in a specific place and at a specific time. They are multi-dimensional phenomena. It is also necessary to recognise the differentiation in the effects of border challenges, with some developments, particularly the neo-liberal economic claims underpinning the 'borderless world' notions of the likes of Ohmae, having greater applicability to the Organisation for Economic Cooperation and Development (OECD) and even here generating backlashes, particularly in terms of identity.[40]

It is important to note that these approaches and ideas in political and critical geography and geo-politics do not appear from nowhere. 'Boundary studies have had a long, descriptive and relatively nontheoretical history in geography.'[41] Thus the lack of concerted attention on territorial borders in international relations reflects the traditional approach in political geography too. In international relations James Rosenau has attempted, though, to develop an idea of the 'frontier' as being the shifting, and sometimes elusive, site of international politics in an era he argues is characterised by a dynamic of 'fragmegration' – an unstable mixture of integrative and fragmenting dynamics. This has substantial implications for territorial borders, leaving them as central at some times and in some places and basically irrelevant in and at others.[42]

Rosenau's arguments are interesting for several reasons, but most important here is the way that he fits into the same kind of practical, policy-oriented, philosophically realist tradition of international relations theory that has dominated the discipline. Rosenau has little time for the post-structuralism of a Tuathail, for example, but he is keen to argue for the conceptual indefensibility of the strictly Westphalian territorial border.

This stems from an analysis of the contemporary dynamics of international relations that are de-centreing the state. This sees certain political functions being integrated in the hands of supranational organisations, of which the European Union (EU) is the most highly developed, but with bodies like the World Trade Organisation, the International Criminal Court (ICC) and the G-8 also fitting into this kind of list. As a result, the distinction between domestic and international politics which Rosenau, as with most realists, assumes to have been pretty sharp in the past is declining.

The possibility of war within organisations like the EU is almost vanishingly small and they no longer conduct their politics on the basis of specialist foreign ministries staffed by diplomats who understand their job as being something set apart from the role of domestic bureaucrats. Instead, the state apparatus is involved across a whole range of issues and government departments in the conduct of relations with other states, forming coalitions not just against other governments, but potentially against other departments of their own government, too. The classic realist notion of the balance of power is difficult to discern in this kind of political arrangement and where the domestic ends and the foreign starts is equally blurred.

Political fragmentation is perhaps the more interesting of the two dynamics for our purposes, though, because it points to ways of thinking about the 'failed' or 'collapsed state' phenomena that is also important in discussions of post-9/11 international politics. Rosenau sees the collapse of the Socialist Federal Republic of Yugoslavia, of Somalia, of Rwanda and, presumably, the more recent collapse of the Democratic Republic of Congo, as creating new 'domestic'/'foreign' definitional problems. For example, and very prominent in post-9/11 discussions, is the potential for such states to become havens for terrorist organisations finding in the vacuum of political authority an ideal environment in which to train recruits, establish bases and plan operations. For foreign powers who may be the target of these plans appealing to the 'government' of the state for assistance in suppressing such organisations, assuming that a government is discernible at all, is likely to be of little help if such a government is unable to make its writ run as far as the capital city's ring road, let alone throughout a state which, like the Democratic Republic of Congo, is the size of Western Europe.[43]

Fragmentation also often stimulates refugee movements as people attempt to escape violence, persecution, economic collapse and the general misery of living in conditions of chaos. A whole host of previously 'domestic' issues become tied up with decisions about how to address fragmentation: for example asylum policy, naturalisation and citizenship policies, welfare policies and discourses about the desirability of assimilation of immigrant groups and the extent of licence to be granted to cultural practices on dress, marriage, diet and so on.[44] Rosenau uses this to question the utility of thinking in terms of 'foreign' and 'domestic' policy categories. Instead, he argues that is along the frontier between these two that we need to focus our attention. This includes, up to a point, the territorial border between the state and the rest of the world and the difficulties of seeing this as a 'natural' barrier between the state and what happens elsewhere, and as a dividing line between different modes and forms of politics.

However, whilst the problems of seeing the line on the map as being of such fundamental importance to how we understand the policy world is recognised in Rosenau's 'fragmegrating' world, the role of the territorial border in delimiting sovereignty appears unchanged. Territorial borders will not disappear and neither will some recognisable notion of sovereignty, even when in the most integrated parts of the world we may have to cope with the mental gymnastics of 'pooled' or 'shared' sovereignty. Equally, the idea of the ethics of territorial borders being a valid question is also absent from Rosenau's view. The territorialisation of international politics continues in a more complicated way, but not in a fundamentally re-conceptualised way.

Beyond this policy-oriented approach to the 'problem' of territorial borders in international relations, work by Campbell[45] and Shapiro and Alker[46] has attempted to stimulate a much more explicitly critical approach to territorial borders. Here the connections, or potential connections, to the trend in political geography are clearest, with Newman and Paasi noting the emerging crossover between critical geo-politics, for example, and critical international relations.[47]

Nevertheless, and as Rosenau notes, in international relations, theorists from the major approaches have failed to properly recognise the idea that 'boundaries have in fact been instruments of communication aimed at reifying, but at the same time depersonalizing, power.'[48] The state as an actor, and in particular the territorial borders that define it, have become 'invisible' in the sense of not being subject to critical analysis. This is despite their massive visibility in the shaping and controlling of the lives of people and their huge importance in one of the core questions of international relations – war and conflict.[49]

The binding of territorial borders into a framework that sees the domestic as the arena of order and control and the external as the site of war and conflict leads us to the kind of 'inside/outside' thinking that has been a mainstay of the post-modern and post-structural critique of established thinking in international relations.[50] This stresses how it is that the construction of a dichotomy between politics within the state and politics between states has developed and helped to sustain a set of social practices around international relations that are highly exclusionary. In particular, the reification of a portrayal of international relations as the realm of military might, of deep insecurity, of perpetual fear of war and as an arena where ethics are, if not entirely absent, then only extremely weakly present has privileged certain social groups and institutions. The military, of course, is the principal beneficiary, but a separate and specialised class of diplomats – 'honest men sent abroad to lie for their country' in Sir Henry Wooton's memorable phrase – has also been created. In particular, this has served to exclude foreign policy from the same sort of political scrutiny and contestation that characterises 'domestic' politics, where such things can be tolerated because the risks are so much reduced. The political appeals to 'bi-partisanship', to rallying around the flag or uniting behind 'our boys' (and, these days, 'girls' as well) remain strong political cards to play.

Many feminist authors have also highlighted the exclusion of women from international relations, reduced to the roles of victims in conflict, 'diplomatic wives', military camp followers and the providers of comfort and reassurance from the 'home front'. Women have been 'domesticated' as it were their political exclusion from the international realm mirroring the feminist critique of the confining of women, and issues of principal concern to women, to the 'private' world in the political discourse within the state and thus not the proper subject of 'public' policy and politics.[51]

The development of international political theory in the last two decades has been characterised by an assault on borders of all sorts, even if the idea of the border or boundary has been used in a metaphorical sense rather than in a territorial one.[52] It has sought to challenge the reification of borders, although more rarely does it engage in a deep-rooted and historical analysis as to why this situation has emerged. This book claims that history is important in developing not just a critical understanding of territorial borders, but also in offering a better account of the ethics of territorial borders.

In large part these developments in international political theory rest upon the dissolution, usually associated with post-positivism, of the boundaries between fact and value, theory and practice that we associate with mainstream social science.[53] This effort to explore, in diverse ways, the socially constructed nature of international politics and to assert the ideational nature of the great majority of what were in the past regarded as 'the facts' of international politics has opened vast swathes of space for ethical enquiry.[54] Three examples will hopefully suffice to illustrate this point and to explain why this move establishes the need for a stronger ethical and normative turn in the ongoing reconsideration of territorial borders.

First, as mentioned earlier, Kimberley Hutchings has asserted the distorting effect on our ethical and normative vision of a deeply entrenched Western philosophical assumption about the essential incommensurability of the worlds of politics and ethics.[55] Under this assumption the boundary lies between different modes of thought and enquiry whereby the practical, pragmatic needs of politics can never be made to fit with the purity and permanence of an idealised ethical situation. Instead, the best that can be hoped for is the insertion into the world of politics of some of the principles of the world of ethics as a way of limiting the more brutal consequences of an untrammelled politics.

Hutchings argues politics need not be ethically neutered and neither are ethics apolitical. Instead there needs to be recognition of a mutually constitutive relationship that is critically dynamic. Once we have accepted the idea that the role and meaning of borders is the product of social practice, as the political geographers argue, we cannot then go on to argue that territorial borders are political necessities, isolated by the nature of politics from ethical enquiry. The idea of a 'pragmatic', 'practical' or 'real' political world that is immunised against or insulated from ethical significance is untenable on the basis of Hutching's argument, and the efforts to pursue politics on the basis of such an argument has resulted in attempts to offer practical justifications for ethically unsustainable action.

This is not to deny the presence of genuine ethical dilemmas in international politics. Indeed, international politics can throw up some of the most difficult dilemmas that political life is capable of generating. Political leaders may indeed be faced with the necessity of making choices, none of which are ethically desirable but at least one of which cannot be ducked. Political leadership can bring with it the kind of responsibility that few people would willingly undertake. However, a recognition of the ethical significance of political action, long advocated in certain quarters in international relations, is necessary to fully appreciate the gravity of choices that leaders may have to make and, one would hope, also a part of the decision-making process itself. There are, of course, political decisions that are taken for all the wrong reasons, or that fall short of what we can realistically expect, but that we are able to identify such choices and that such a critique has political power is in itself a testament to the way that ethics are a part of international politics. To follow Ken Booth's point here, we know that human rights exist in international politics because we can point to human wrongs.[56]

Secondly, the post-positivist turn has enabled another boundary to be challenged: that between domestic and international politics.[57] From the international side of the border-as-fence, it is no longer feasible to view the border as marking the place beyond which ethics start, and therefore rendering ethics as being of little interest to a properly international perspective.[58] Instead, the role of borders in generating such bifurcation in our perceptions of ethics becomes a vital part of the enquiry into them. If the 'outside' is really 'in', and the 'inside' really 'out', then how and why it has proved possible to maintain the distinction for so long is an important question. It also makes the conceptualisation and ethical content of territorial borders an inescapable topic of enquiry. In particular, recognising the importance of power in constructing this understanding and recognising the ways in which the social practices tied up in borders suit certain power-holding groups not only brings critical perspectives to bear, but reminds us of the inevitability of creating borders through social practice.

The response to 9/11 carries with it elements of this desire to dismantle the domestic/international divide. This is most obvious in the concern shown about the domestic politics of a number of regimes and their potential or actual proclivity to harbour terrorists. However, 'the axis of evil' is a fairly cheap rhetorical shot, the kind of phrase that livens up a speech and sticks in the memory – as shown by the frequency with which it is repeated, including here.

More thoughtful, though is the way that notions of responsibility have been argued over and the way that linkages between domestic and international politics have been made in this regard.

At one level we see this in the kind of critique of US foreign policy, especially towards the Middle East, that has caused some to see the United States as author of its own downfall, or at least the downfall of the 'twin towers'. Elshtain is bitterly critical of this kind of argument, at least in its crude, 'America had it coming', form, because she sees this as absolving terrorists of moral responsibility for their actions, and that this cannot be done. The wilful destruction of the World Trade Centre and the attempted destruction of the Pentagon amount to acts of mass murder and that this can never be a legitimate response to the policies of any state. Elshtain also argues that poverty, ignorance, hopelessness and alienation are equally invalid as excuses for such action, although they may have a role to play in explanation. Again, the issue of accepting responsibility is important here, and that this can, indeed must, be judged against criteria that are meaningfully universal, no matter how twisted by religious fundamentalism.

However, Elshtain does recognise a connection between the domestic and the international in her analysis of political and ethical responsibility. This comes in the way that she connects the existence of 'ordinary civic peace' within the state to the existence of something similar between states. If we are to enjoy the basis for the creation of a culture that recognises and respects notions such as justice, rights, toleration, human dignity and so on within the state then we need the possibility for such things to exist between states, too. A state that is constantly menaced by the 'war of all against all' supposed to lie at the root of the international condition will be unable to create such civic peace because it will permanently be having to impose exceptional security measures and burden its citizens with the needs of military service. Maintaining some kind of 'international society', as we shall see in more detail in Chapter 3, thus becomes an ethically important goal of state policy because without this a civil society at home becomes unsustainable.[59]

Elshtain's argument here is used to support her justification of military action against Afghanistan and Iraq in the wake of 9/11. It is part of what I have called the 'rush to the state' that Elshtain's book appears to me to typify: that in the face of these kinds of threats and challenges it is to the state that we must turn to offer us not just security, in the sense of being the most powerful and effective institution to combat terrorism, but also the basis for creating civil societies that will be inimical to radical, and especially radically religious, politics of hate and destruction.

To the kind of post-structural analysis that started this critique of the domestic/international divide, though, this kind of argument will seem to be part of a re-legitimation of the power of the state and, most importantly, of the state's elites. The idea that the fear of terrorism has been exaggerated in order to provide political leaders with an opportunity and excuse to introduce draconian, anti-libertarian and even racist legal measures under the rubric of 'national security' is reasonably widespread.[60] It links to the analysis of the culture of national security exemplified by David Campbell's work on the ways in which the culture of security in the United States in particular has been constructed and manipulated in ways that help to sustain existing structures of social power and preserve the authority of the institutions of national security.[61] The fear of terrorism and the threat of certain governments hostile to the interests on the major powers are therefore liable to be exaggerated or, to borrow a phrase that is perhaps apposite in these circumstances, 'sexed up'.[62]

The merits of this case, and the evidence to sustain or refute it, are not really the concern here though. It does show how it is that theoretical arguments about the ways in which the domestic/international divide is constructed are coming through in political debate, which is what is important here. There is another level at which the domestic/international divide is being challenged, though, as part of the post-9/11 debates and this is the way that globalisation and transnational terrorism are being connected.

Arguments put forward by the British government, and particularly by Tony Blair as Prime Minister, are good examples of this. Blair made the case, as part of his justifications for war against Iraq, that 9/11 had changed fundamentally the nature of security in the world and, in particular, the ways that globalisation is transforming not just the economic circumstances of the world but also the security situation. In particular, it makes the domestic/international divide unsustainable because of the way that terrorist organisations are able to make use of the same kinds of networks that sustain the web of transnational trade, finance and investment that makes the global economy work. Where they are able to find governments willing to support them or where there are collapsed or failed states then this becomes all the easier, making the domestic politics of such states a subject of legitimate international concern. Blair explicitly linked this idea to globalisation, drawing a direct analogy between the transformation that globalisation is bringing to the world's economic systems and structures and that which terrorism is bringing to the security situation.[63]

Targeting terrorist organisations exploiting these changed global security circumstances is thus difficult to do whilst maintaining a strict domestic/international divide. Instead, the character of governments becomes a crucial security question, with Blair pushing the idea that brutal, repressive, WMD-desiring regimes like Saddam Hussein's are amongst the most important security threats in the world today. This category could presumably be extended to include regimes portrayed as pro-terrorist religious fundamentalists, like the Taliban, or collapsed, chaotic power vacuums like that in Somalia. Fortunately, a combination of all three is seriously unlikely to come about. Nevertheless, the politics of states cannot be bracketed out as a 'domestic' matter and thus none of the business of the rest of the world.

The third area in which international political theory has contributed to opening the question of the ethics of territorial borders follows directly from the questioning of the domestic/international divide as one kind of intellectual border. Challenging the fact/value and inside/outside boundaries has, in turn, seen new boundaries erected and challenged. Perhaps the most significant in developing international political theory has been the idea of an important distinction between communitarian and cosmopolitan approaches to making ethical judgement.[64] Communitarianism can be seen as being linked to defending the right of a specific political community, often a territorially bounded and idealised nation, to a substantial degree of ethical closure.[65] Cosmopolitanism, on the other hand, argues in favour of a universal ethical schema, enabling us to make meaningful and politically important judgements about the ethics of actions and ideas wherever they may occur. The most common basis of cosmopolitanism is probably liberalism, indeed the debate is sometimes referred to as the 'liberal–communitarian' debate, but the label cosmopolitanism is preferred here because of the way that it enables non-liberal universalism to be admitted. The influence of the influx of political philosophy into international relations is clear in this debate, with both camps often associated with towering figures of European political philosophy, Hegel and Kant.[66]

Substantial efforts to overcome this boundary exist. Andrew Linklater cites both Kant and Hegel as important influences in his effort to develop a cosmopolitan ethic for international relations, one that simultaneously advocates a greater sense of shared humanity whilst extending communal sensitivity in a more distributively just world.[67] Mervyn Frost is another who attempts to utilise Hegelian method in the service of cosmopolitan aims, focused on the constitution of individuals as rights-holders within a nexus of social situations, including the sovereign state and the states-system.[68]

However, both these approaches, and the need to make the cosmopolitan/communitarian distinction central, have been challenged. Hutchings argues that their divergence from or solutions to this problem are generally unsuccessful, 'collapsing back' into one or other of these dichotomised camps.[69] Molly Cochran offers a particularly useful source of critique of this border in international political theory for our purposes, because of the way she highlights ontological questions in this regard. She has argued that even without the bold philosophical and methodological certainties of Enlightenment positivism, both cosmopolitan and communitarian camps have made 'strong', too strong in her view, claims about ethical standards in international relations.[70] The ontological foundations of the competing camps cannot, she asserts, be sustained. The power of the post-positivist critique is sufficient, in Cochran's view, to require us to hold as few ontological assumptions as weakly as possible, constantly recognising them as assumptions, rather than facts, and holding open the possibility of change at all times. Thus, the epistemological conclusions that Linklater and Frost reach about valid ethical knowledge are highly questionable, because what Cochran sees as being their weak ontological foundations nevertheless yield non-contingent judgements about ethical principle and process.[71]

Cochran instead appeals to a philosophical pragmatism indebted to Dewey and Rorty as an alternative way around this problem.[72] She urges such a course on the grounds of maximising the potential for ethical discourse and inclusiveness.[73] Ontological characterisation, for Cochran, closes avenues of enquiry by defining them out of existence, or at least out of admissibility in ethical debate. Those holding views incompatible with privileged ontological positions are silenced and marginalised.[74] Cochran's sparsely populated ontological world offers great room for manoeuvre, debate and discussion amongst diverse and divergent ethical perspectives. It is these benefits that she stresses, so that the necessary ontological assumptions are those that enable entry to such an environment and the bringing of a perspective to share. She argues that an ironically held liberalism offers the best approach, in that liberalism has demonstrated a pragmatic ability to be open to alternatives, to be dynamic in its ethical agenda and to offer ways of safe-guarding diversity and individuality. If this can be stripped of foundational ideas, such as sovereign individuality, then such a liberal sensibility and respect for diversity and individuality offers an ideal, although contingently ideal, ethical framework.[75]

A greater ethical inclusiveness certainly further undermines the idea of territorial borders as delimiting zones of exclusive authority, ownership and identity. By extension, this ought also to lead to discussions of ethical inclusion. However, whilst geographers like Newman have emphasised the ongoing and dynamic role of borders in constituting and re-constituting identity, this ethical turn has not been fully taken.[76] '[A] rich understanding of the ways in which power is embedded in social space has developed...yet little attention is given to normative implications, to how things ought to be different.'[77] For example, Tuathail's 'critical geopolitics' certainly seeks to exploit fully the potential for post-positivist critique of borders as taken-for-granted, natural and immutable facts of the sovereign states-system. However, this is at the cost of a neglect of ethics' concern with exploring the progressive traits immanent in existing practice and the need to be sensitive to the powerful sense of right and wrong embedded in existing practice and deeply valued by individuals and communities. David M. Smith notes that geography's engagement with ethics in recent years has produced a range of responses, but no '... core activity to which the label of geography and ethics can sensibly be assigned'.[78] Given the range, depth and importance of the ethical issues surrounding territorial borders, this could be the core that Smith is searching for.

Tuathail's approach certainly could be a way into this, but as with other work taking its inspiration from Derrida and Foucault, it is subject to similar charges levelled at Cochran's ontological minimalism.

By removing all, or very nearly all, the props of our conceptualisation and understanding of situations and institutions the risks of ethical relativism appear. If there are no standards that matter – because ultimately all are the products of a power understood as coercive, repressive and factional – then power is all there is. We should no longer be surprised, let alone ethically troubled, that the world has been made by the powerful and will be re-made in the future by the powerful because it could not be any other way. The ethical standards, whether evidenced or immanent in practice and institutions, inevitably lose their meaning. Radicalism can become cynicism or even paranoia about existing practice, regarding it as all being the result of the imposition by the strong upon the weak of norms that masquerade self-interest and the protection of structures of power as speaking to chimerical wider and genuine notions of the good.[79]

Efforts to critique the geographical reification of borders and expand inclusiveness are concerned with strategies and techniques for overcoming the divisiveness associated with territorial borders. International political theory has focused on their role in the idea that 'foreigners' – those who live or originate from beyond the borders of our state – are none of our ethical concern. However, whilst so keen on re-conceptualising so many of the dividing lines of thought and ethical category, international political theorists have not fully employed the attention lavished on the dividing lines on the map by critical political geography. For them territorial borders seem to endure, but a more inclusive ethic will be able to work around or across them.

This points to one of the themes of the next chapter of the book – the idea that territorial borders ought to take on an ethically contingent status. They have no ethical standing in and of themselves, instead they are institutionalised social practices whose value is determined by how they contribute, or not, to the attainment of a higher ethical purpose, assuming one can be found.[80] This is something the book seeks to challenge, but it is a powerful and interesting argument, and one that will be explored in some detail in Chapter 3. It is worth pointing out, though, that the contingency argument has been heard quite loudly in international politics in recent years, as governments and other actors have sought to respond to the challenges of humanitarian intervention and the war on terror. The International Commission on Intervention and State Sovereignty (ICISS), in their important report on humanitarian intervention, Responsibility to Protect, argue strongly, especially in the first half of the report, that sovereignty and the protection of the non-intervention norm should be contingent on government's effectively fulfilling their responsibility to protect the basic rights of citizens. Where such protection is absent, either through the collapse of effective authority or through deliberate and large-scale flouting of those rights, then the responsibility to protect may pass to the rest of the international community, and this may require forcible intervention.

Similarly, the Bush Administration's response to 9/11 also aims to make it clear that it regards effective counter-terrorist action by governments as a condition of respecting their sovereignty. Harbouring terrorism is equated with terrorism itself and such states are cast into the category of 'enemy', the potential subject of preventative war.[81] This is the rhetorical position, at least, but it does represent a strong challenge to the 'Westphalian' position of sovereignty and calls into doubt the idea that what takes place within the territorial borders of a state is essentially none of the business of the rest of the world, unless this generates an imminent threat of direct military attack, or is declared a threat to international peace and security by the UN Security Council. George W. Bush's ultimatum to the UN in September 2002 to accept the US understanding of the issues of Iraq and terrorism and act on that basis or risk becoming irrelevant is symptomatic of the desire to change the established understanding of the rights and privileges that attach to sovereignty and render them contingent in new ways.[82]

The appreciation of territorial borders as dynamic norms and their more careful and thorough consideration as social phenomena combines with boundary challenging international political theory to produce strategies for thinking through the ethical implications of borders-as-fences. Contingency is one approach, but before we can conclude in its favour we need to take a step backward. Bringing these two strands of critique together asks some hard prior questions about the ontology of borders, if we wish to avoid relativism, and the role of ontology in ethics. These need developing if we are to adopt the most appropriate way of thinking through the ethics of borders.

The ontology of borders and the need for ontological choices

As Hutchings stresses, trying to set the world of ethics aside from the world of politics has unacceptable intellectual and practical costs.[83] There is a need for a critical re-examination of what 'is' in the search for what 'ought to be'. Part of this, though, should also be to recognise the existing ontological status of elements of an international ethic. If we need to start from where we are, part of that is also about recognising the relative fixity and sedimentation of different parts of where we are. A radical ontological minimalism brings with it the benefit of opening ethical space, but if this can only be explored in a way that relies on the detachment from where we are necessary to such an ontology then the difficulties of situating ethical enquiry re-appear. Rather than the search for an unobtainable ethical Archimedean point, ontological minimalism searches for an equally unobtainable point requiring similar levels of detachment from the inter-subjective, transitory and contextual ethical world that is the starting point for critical interrogation.

Many studies accept that territorial borders occupy a strong onto-logical position in understandings of international relations.[84] Thus an enquiry into their ethical role ought to recognise this level of entrenchment and the general acceptance of their role to the point that such roles are rarely questioned. As Ruggie says, 'Some constitutive rules, like exclusive territoriality, are so deeply sedimented or reified that actors no longer think of them as rules at all.'[85] That sedimentation and reification which characterise the situation should also play a role in our enquiry. Sayer and Storper 'acknowledge the extraordinary durability of the spatial material forms in which inequalities and injustices are embedded.'[86] This raises questions as to how and why it is that this situation has come about and to what sort of ethical principles or needs does it speak. This is an important addition to enquiring into the social, economic and political, often power-political, roles stressed in fields such as critical geo-politics. If 'It goes without saying that if a boundary exists, something must be enclosed within it',[87] then that something can be the source of ethical value and normative vision, as well as the product of power. If Hutchings is correct and power and ethics ought not to be and cannot be divided into their separate realms then there is a need to recognise that power can also be right and right can also be powerful.

An immanent critique therefore requires us to move away from ontological minimalism, raising prior questions about how this should be done. '[P]recisely because there are micro- and macrogeographies of power, normative proposals must be highly sensitive to these flows and sedimented forms, and not fall prey to a facile kind of utopianism.'[88] The dangers of over-compensating, though, are clear – that by accepting the status of existing institutions as a part of our starting point we potentially re-legitimise their established and dominant position, producing *post facto* justifications for the status quo.[89] A critical ethical edge is essential but it needs to be found within existing practice, or at least to be seen to be a possible development within existing practice.

Given the dominance of the territorial borders-as-fences-between-states perspective, it is necessary to adopt an approach that takes the strength of this conception seriously, but without repeating the mistake of reification. Treating territorial borders as social practices importantly connected to power and ethics, vital to the construction and maintenance of states and an interstate system across time, points to the need to use the history of statehood. This needs to avoid seeing states and their borders as inevitable or automatically superior, but that helps us appreciate how they have become so ubiquitous and embedded in international politics.

One way this has been explored historically, and in a methodologically post-positivist way, is by Hendrik Spruyt.[90] He points to the state's origins in France in response to changing trading and economic conditions from the twelfth century onwards and how it proved to be more effective in the new conditions than its competitors, the City League and the City State.[91] Spruyt emphasises the role of a specific understanding of territory and especially the specific and sharp delimitation of ownership as important to the success of the state in competition with these alternative forms.[92] It is the domestic organisational and economic benefits brought by this approach to territory that he asserts as being at least as, if not more, important than the war-making ability of states.[93] Thus war and the struggle for survival are not the only explanations for the triumph of the state.[94] The classic and most frequently critiqued aspect of state power is not the end of the story.

This sort of 'neo-classical constructivism', to borrow a label of Ruggie's, plays to our needs and its choice is thus a pragmatic one, rather than a claim about its necessary methodological superiority.[95] Given that territorial borders are inextricably bound to the modern sovereign state and the modern sovereign state is inextricably bound to understandings of international relations, ethical critique needs to recognise the ontological status of territorial borders. There is a need for an approach that is comfortable with, but critical of, this and that can appreciate that borders are dynamic social structures.

In the terms of Finnemore and Sikkink, territorial borders-as-fences are a norm that 'cascaded' a long time ago, especially in Europe.[96] By the idea of a norm cascade, Finnemore and Sikkink argue that international norms spread by a process whereby certain actors take on the role of 'norm entrepreneurs', promoting a revision to the existing norms of the international community. When these entrepreneurs are able to attract enough other actors to their view, including some of the leading powers, then the norm reaches a 'tipping point'. From here, the momentum behind it is enough to cause it to 'cascade' throughout the international system, being rapidly adopted and internalised by a large majority of actors. Once a cascade takes place, then practical questions dominate discussions such as, in this case, the location of borders and agreed ways of demarcating and maintaining that location.[97]

The idea of borders-as-fences has not been successfully replaced by an alternative conception. However, this is not to say that cascaded norms do not undergo subsequent evolution and incremental development. Big normative changes in previously acceptable practice may be attention grabbing, but 'mini-cascades' also take place within the general parameters of well-established norms. For example, the shift from an absolutist conception of sovereignty to a popular, national one altered the legitimation of territorial borders – turning them from the delimiter of royal property to the boundaries of national homeland – without substantially altering their role as fences in international politics.[98]

Nicholas Wheeler has used the idea of norm entrepreneurship to look at the idea of humanitarian intervention, exploring the ways in which NATO military action against Serbia during 1999 might be understood as an act of norm entrepreneurship.[99] It is not much of a leap of imagination to see the arguments over the war on terror in a similar light. Ideas put forward by the UK and US governments are not identical in this regard, but they can both be read in these terms to some profit. Thus, for example, the claims made by the United Kingdom about the connections between globalisation, WMD proliferation and the spread of transnational terrorism are about floating a modified understanding of the context of international security.[100] From this flow a number of normative propositions about the connections between the domestic character and behaviour of states and an entitlement to the protection of the non-intervention norm. With this comes a reconsideration of the norms attached to the idea of a territorial border that helps to downgrade the normative significance of the Westphalian notion of a border.

The US government's position is somewhat different, with attention there having focused on the idea of preventative war.[101] Again, this can be read as an effort to persuade other states to accept an adjustment to the norms that frame our understanding of the use of force in international relations. Acceptance of a norm of preventative war is very strongly resisted by some, who argue that one of the major achievements of international society, especially in the last hundred years or so, has been to more and more tightly restrict the circumstances in which war is a legitimate response. The UN Charter position is something to be protected whereby self-defence and collective action, under the authority of the Security Council, in response to a threat to international peace and security are the only legitimate grounds for war. The argument runs that loosening the definition of self-defence to allow preventative action, as the Bush Administration has proposed, risks opening the flood gates to a whole raft of 'preventative' wars pursued for a great range of motives and with potentially massively de-stabilising consequences for international politics. Territorial borders would lose their role in helping to tentatively define international crimes such as aggression and in helping international society identify when self-defence comes into play, because the armed forces of one state have crossed into another, for example. In an era of preventative war as a general norm any military activity that could conceivably be some sort of preparation for military action against another state could attract a preventative response. The security dilemma would become impossibly acute.

What this idea of norm entrepreneurship shows, within the context of a constructivist methodological framework, is that we can overcome the dangers of an overly static approach that unjustifiably privileges the status quo as an embodiment of the good because of its ability to endure. Equally, it helps to sensitise us to the idea that repeated incremental changes can add up to important normative shifts and can reflect arguments for major changes in the conceptualisation of key elements of the international political system, like territorial borders. Finnnemore and Sikkink's notion of norm cascades tends to emphasise the big, eye-catching changes, and their approach may also be overly formal. Their model is rather too neat for the more organic and untidy ways in which social facts are constructed and re-constructed. This point is particularly important as incremental alterations within established parameters can nevertheless be highly significant. It is essential to recognise this to maintain a critical edge and avoid reinforcing the reification of borders-as-fences that Ruggie highlights.

There is thus a need to situate the kind of model Finnemore and Sikkink propose alongside a more hermeneutic or interpretivist approach to territorial borders. This has the added advantage of avoiding one of the dangers of more formal models in that they tend to reinforce objectivism in study, underplaying the ways in which studying and modelling international politics are also acts of international politics. This is a key post-positivist insight and one that efforts by neo-classical constructivists to reach out to positivist enquiry can overlook too much.[102] Potential transformation is always immanent and norms are always dynamic, even if only through their re-creation, and this can take forms different to those that may have brought the norm into existence as an important element of the ideational structure of the international system.

Thus a more hermeneutic approach to norms in constructivism offers an account of the normatively charged and ethically important role of the rules, norms and principles of behaviour that states have evolved through practice over a substantial historical period. It is possible to engage in a critical ethical investigation of territorial borders-as-fences that reflects the ontological sedimentation of these foundational elements of the international system, but that does not have to become an apologia for the status quo. Ontological assumptions are essential to any enquiry and they ought to be self-consciously made. However, a post-positivist ethics interrogating the immanent ethical potential of the world as it has been constructed needs these assumptions to reflect the here and now.

Conclusion

This chapter has tried to show how developments in political geography, critical geo-politics and international political theory have helped to open up academic enquiry into territorial borders. This is less eye-catching that the grand claims of a borderless world, or similar, predicated on more empirical and practical developments, but they are just as important if we are to think seriously about the ethics of territorial borders. The questioning of territorial borders is important and has potentially far-reaching consequences for how we think, or ought to think, about the ethical aspects of their role in international relations. The work in political geography has demonstrated how the essentialised, border-as-fence conception is both inadequate and misleading, particularly in terms of naturalising and de-politicising one of the most powerful and potent political symbols. Post-positivist ethics has nevertheless sensitised us to the need to search for and be aware of immanent ethical potential in practice and the need for a situated ethics that comes from, rather than is separate to, social and political practices, including power. The depth of the sedimentation of the border-as-fence analogy in international politics caused us to question the more ontologically minimalist approaches to international ethics as being an appropriate mechanism for considering the ethics of territorial borders.

The suggestion put forward so far is that debates about contemporary political issues, such as humanitarian intervention and the war on terror, can be usefully seen in this light. The proposals and arguments are not just about the best way to address these political challenges, they have deeper resonance and significance because of the way that they potentially re-conceptualise territorial borders, amongst other things. One way in which this is occurring, we have seen, is through the idea of contingency – that respect for territorial borders becomes contingent on the willingness and ability of a government to abide by certain standards and expectations, mainly in relation to human rights and counter-terrorism. This contingency is not new, of course, the Westphalian notion of territorial borders carries with it a degree of contingency – on states abiding by the rules of diplomacy, of reciprocating the recognition of sovereignty and the rights and duties that go along with that, and so on.

This locates territorial borders within what has been referred to as an 'international society'. This takes its theoretical framing from the English school of international relations theory and it is in this direction that we turn in Chapter 3. However, it is important to note that the English school has also undergone something of a renewal of interest in the last 10 years or so, alongside the interest in territorial borders. This has been importantly methodological, with efforts being made to reconsider both what Hedley Bull called the 'classical' method on thinking about international relations, most importantly re-stated by Robert Jackson, and ways to connect the English school to post-positivism.[103] The latter has, in my opinion, been much more successful and has substantially sharpened the critical edge that English school theory has been able to deploy. In particular, the connection to the wider currents of social theory fits well with the approach set out here, and enables the English school to play an important part in the ethical reconsideration of territorial borders.

One particularly pertinent development has been the interest in cosmopolitan, or 'solidarist' to use the English school term, ethical frameworks and normative propositions. This has been importantly driven by the role that English school writers have played in the academic examination of the problem of humanitarian intervention. The focus here has been the tensions between Westphalian notions of sovereignty and universalistic claims about humanity, human rights and humanitarianism that have been prominent in calls to effectively address crises such as those in the former Yugoslavia, Somalia, Rwanda, East Timor, Haiti and elsewhere.

English school advocates of a more cosmopolitan normative agenda have seen the development of serious discussion about a right to humanitarian intervention in international relations as marking a potentially highly significant change in the ethics of international relations. This moves away from a very strong defence of an ethic of order predicated on Westphalian notions of sovereignty and a belief in the ethical diversity of the international system towards a view where universal notions of justice have more purchase and can, in extremes, overrule sovereignty. The idea of an emerging 'world society' importantly based on a sense of common feeling amongst human beings as human beings is an important part of this argument.[104] The challenging of reified, essentialised and static notions of territorial borders is one element of this dynamic, and thus one reason why it is of interest here.

The main focus of our discussion of the English school's ideas, though, is on the way that arguments like these reinforce the notion of the contingency of territorial borders that we have seen coming through in public policy debates about humanitarian intervention and the war on terror. The English school is thus a useful framework for exploring the possibility that the ethics of territorial borders can be thought of in terms of contingency. The way in which territorial borders have been constructed in Westphalian terms, and the ways in which arguments about humanitarian intervention and the war on terror are challenging this construction, can be judged on the basis of the contingency of borders. They possess ethical standing only because they are elements of an institutional structure that serves some higher ethical goal.

As already indicated, this is an argument that the book wishes to ultimately reject, but that does not mean it can be ignored. The power and political appeal of the contingency argument is significant and, as suggested, it has clear echoes in contemporary policy debates about the changing nature of international politics. It also serves as a very useful way of introducing some important liberal arguments into this debate, following on from the idea that challenges to territorial borders as fences are a part of a cosmopolitan or solidarist normative agenda that takes a great deal of its political philosophical groundings from a liberal view of politics. Most significantly, it is a way to discuss the question of rights in the context of territorial borders, as the idea, or ideal, of universal human rights is perhaps the clearest way of establishing the contingency of territorial borders on cosmopolitan grounds, offering a stark contrast to the older English school argument in favour of interstate order.

It is thus time to move on and look at how the critical perspective we have opened on territorial borders through these methodological manoeuvres helps underpin arguments about the role of territorial borders in promoting higher ethical goals, such as order and justice, the relationship between them, and how one way through what appears to be a potentially irreconcilable conflict still leaves territorial borders ethically contingent.

3
The Ethical Contingency of Territorial Borders?

Introduction

The idea and practice of 'humanitarian intervention' is one of the most important issues to have emerged in international politics in the last 15 years, and has been the subject of a great deal of academic enquiry as well as practical political debate.[1] This is not a book about humanitarian intervention, but the arguments about the nature, purpose and desirability of the development of a right, or possibly even a duty, of humanitarian intervention have a direct impact on the ways in which we understand the role of territorial borders in international politics and, most importantly here, about their ethical status.

The war on terror has added to this debate. Some of these additions, such as discussions of the impact on sovereignty, are potentially compatible with the propositions of those in favour of a limited right to humanitarian intervention, and receive the bulk of the attention here.[2] Some governments, such as Tony Blair's in the United Kingdom, have even attempted to make an explicit connection between the two, reiterating arguments in favour of military action against Iraq in 2003, for example, first made in defence of military action against the Federal Republic of Yugoslavia in 1999 in response to the crisis in Kosovo.[3] Other elements of the war on terror are much harder to see as fitting into a general set of claims about sovereignty linking humanitarian intervention and the war on terror. For example, the emphasis placed by the US administration on preventative military action, unilaterally where necessary, and its arguments for a far more permissive re-interpretation of the meaning of 'self-defence' under Article 51 of the UN Charter, would seem to be sharply at odds with the strongly multi-lateralist stance of the supporters of humanitarian intervention.[4]

Why both are of interest to thinking about the ethics of territorial borders, though, is because of the ways that they challenge the consensus that we saw in Chapter 2 about the idea of territorial borders-as-fences. Materialist accounts of territorial borders see this as just being the way things are and that the challenges of humanitarian intervention and the war on terror may well founder on the rocks of the hard realities of the structure of international politics. As a result, policy responses to situations such as that in the run up to the 2003 war against Iraq ought to be seen in the same light as security questions of the past, with similar kinds of solutions proposed. Thus, to take a prominent example, leading neo-realist figures in the United States dismissed the need for preventative military action in the case of Iraq, rejecting the Bush administration's arguments that 9/11 had fundamentally altered the nature of security challenges and thus required new policy mechanisms. Instead, they argued, Saddam Hussein presented the same kind of threat to United States and Middle East security that he had since the late 1980s and consequently the mechanisms of deterrence and containment that had proven themselves effective during the 1990s should be persisted with.[5]

However, this kind of analysis appeals to a material conception of the structure of the international system in which territorial borders play fixed, immutable and security-centred roles. We have already seen how territorial borders are better understood as social practices, rather than material facts, and thus it is necessary to consider seriously the possibility of change in the role that they play in international politics. This is not, of course, to simply and unquestioningly accept the rhetoric of the US, UK or other governments, but it would be just as mistaken to disregard the possibility of change. The challenges that humanitarian intervention and the war on terror represent for traditional conceptions are potentially of fundamental significance to the role, status and prominence of territorial borders and, our main concern here, to the ethical role of these institutions of international politics.

Whilst the concept and practices of sovereignty are usually in the spotlight in these kinds of enquiries, the debate has tended to become somewhat static, with little way through what seem on the face of it to be incompatible positions defending either the primacy of some form of cosmopolitan ethical schema mandating humanitarianism, or a defence of sovereignty, sometimes linked to the rights of political communities, mandating a much more restrictive position.[6] The ground that is left to debate between these two is whether or not some sort of pragmatic framework can be developed that will enable decisions to be taken about where and when to intervene on a basis that is generally applicable, reasonably intellectually coherent and widely politically acceptable. The prime candidate for providing such a framework is the Just War tradition, modified in certain key areas to better fit the kinds of problems that humanitarian crises present.[7] Just War thinking has also been prominent in discussions of how to deal with global terrorism in the aftermath of 9/11, with both defences and criticisms of the military action taken in Afghanistan, Iraq and elsewhere appealing to Just War categories.[8] Efforts to radically alter these categories have generally resulted in proponents being subjected to some powerful rebuttals by defenders of more orthodox positions.[9]

Looking at territorial borders may help us to break out of this kind of debate about the status of sovereignty and the need to navigate some kind of pragmatic middle ground between essentially irreconcilable positions. This is because of the way that it can enable better ways of thinking about bordering as a social practice and the role that bordering behaviour plays in ethical thinking. This is, though, a rather counter-intuitive position in many regards and it is necessary to explore more thoroughly the ways in which the debate is usually framed in order to see why these approaches have proven to be not entirely successful in enabling ethical thinking about humanitarian intervention and the war on terror that is coherent, effective and practical.

The starting point for this enquiry is the so-called 'English school' of international relations theory. This is a useful place to start because of the way that the English school is potentially methodologically in-tune with the approach laid out in Chapter 2, or, at the very least, is methodologically pluralist enough for this approach not to create insurmountable obstacles.[10] Secondly, an English school account offers us a way of engaging directly with the ethical questions that are important here because of the way that it contains a tension between pluralist and solidarist normative schemas and the connection between these two and the ethically significant concepts of order and justice in international politics.[11] Thirdly, the general thrust of the debate in English school thinking in response to humanitarian intervention in particular has been to stress the solidarist or ethically cosmopolitan opportunities that are available and to see this as a way to re-balance the relationship between order and justice in a way that places greater emphasis on justice. This is generally cast in a broadly liberal way, using ideas such as universal human rights, civil society and democracy, as prominent parts of the argument about both how international politics is changing and how it ought to change.[12] This leads to a fourth benefit of approaching this question from an English school direction – namely that it opens up a series of questions about the state, and especially a liberal understanding of the state.[13] These are vital to establishing the idea of the ethical contingency of territorial borders that we seek to explore in this chapter, and to a potential, if ultimately unsatisfactory, defence of territorial borders on the grounds that they serve an ethic that stresses rights and duties of special beneficence as a way to limit and render practicable the concept of rights and the conceptualisation of the state in a rights-based international political system.[14] However, this, as with its order-emphasising counter-part in the English school, results in the ethical contingency of territorial borders, a position this book seeks to refute.

Thus the chapter progresses by first setting out in rough outline the English school's claims, focusing on the tensions between order and justice, pluralism and solidarism, as being at the core of the ethical tension in the school's position. From here we move on to look at how the debate between pluralism and solidarism has tended to come to a standstill when contained within the framework of international society, looking at how pluralists reject solidarist claims and with them normative projects for a universal approach to justice. The chapter then looks at how arguments about globalisation enable a move away from privileging international society as our conceptual framework, and how this may advance the solidarist cause. In particular, this section stresses the notion of the ethical contingency of territorial borders, using the notion of rights and duties of special beneficence to illustrate how it is that this kind of position can be adopted without producing an argument that

ethically demands the abolition of territorial borders and the creation of a global society. This serves an illustrative function, as there
are other ways of producing an ethical argument that does not make
an end to territorial borders almost inescapable, and some brief
consideration will be given to these. From here we can finally move
to look at the problems with this argument from the perspective of
offering a serious analysis of the ethics of territorial borders, and
especially the way that such projects sidestep the question of territorial
borders by treating them as ethically contingent and failing to
engage fully with the social practice that borders are, instead seeing
them as mere by-products.

The English school, international society and territorial borders

The English school offers us a useful route to discussing the ethical
status of territorial borders and how they may be understood in relation
to contemporary political practice. As discussed above, this is
important in the context of a constructivist methodological approach,
because of the way that we need to treat with due consideration
extremely well-established and entrenched patterns of social practice
and the ways in which we need to search for immanent ethical possibilities in existing practices. In some regards, though, the English
school may not look like a terribly good prospect for this critical
endeavour. It certainly possesses a reputation for a rather conservative approach to understanding international politics. It can be
seen as wary of change and fixated with the state at a time of global
political change that is throwing up new actors, new dynamics and
new political forms that its conceptual framework and theoretical
schema is ill-prepared to engage with. Indeed, a good deal of effort
has recently gone into making the English school's approach to
theory and the structure of its theoretical claims far more systematic
and rigorous.[15] It is certainly true to argue that the notion of international society, or the society of states, that lies at the heart of English
school thinking ontologically privileges the state. In many works,
especially from the earlier period of the school's work, culminating
with Hedley Bull's *The Anarchical Society*, a near-material view of
territorial borders, is the result.[16] If the basic condition of the existence
of international relations is the existence of the Westphalian state

then we would appear to be stuck with the kind of approach to borders that this book has been so critical of.

However, this need not be the case. Whilst writers like Bull, James Mayall and Robert Jackson tend to see the post-Second World War constellation of international society as being very stable, and also largely desirable when alternatives are considered, English school theory is unavoidably committed through its theoretical schema to the ongoing dynamism of international politics.[17]

The English school's portrayal of international relations rests on a tripartite model of ways in which this form of social activity might be framed.[18] The realist or Hobbesian form is characterised by competing pressures pushing in the direction of a brutal game of power politics, where states are little more than egoistic security maximisers, restrained in their behaviour only by the balance of power and temporary coincidences of interest between themselves and other states. The social practices involved here fail to rise much above the level of interaction significant enough that the states have to take one another into account when making decisions – Bull's definition of an international system.[19]

The second model is of a rule and norm-governed pattern of behaviour producing certain minimum social goods, the most important of which, both to the English school and to the argument of this book, is order: '...a pattern of human activity that sustains elementary, primary or universal goals of social life'.[20] Again states are central to this model, but they have been able to create an 'international society' that is able to provide secure enough foundations of shared rules, norms and principles of behaviour that sufficient trust exists for co-operative activity like trade to be possible. Additionally, a reasonably secure level of order also enables ethical questions such as issues of justice to gain a toe-hold on the political agenda. This postion is usually labelled 'rationalist', with the name of the seventeenth-century Dutch jurist Hugo Grotius often attached to this portrayal of international society. Interestingly, though, Edward Keene has persuasively argued this may not be a wholly satisfactory interpretation of either Grotius's writings on international politics, or of the historical record of the expansion of international society.[21] Others, such as Andrew Hurrell, also suggest that the label 'Grotian' ought to be limited to a specific form of international society – one in which there is wide-ranging consensus on certain basic ethical questions.[22]

The third model, generally labelled 'revolutionist', refers to the idea of a 'world society'. This is a universalist political form in which a multiplicity of actors, including individual human beings, participate and where there is a general recognition and acceptance of a common community of human beings. This may include universal ethical propositions, leading to the attachment of the name of Immanuel Kant to this form. Very confusingly from a political theory perspective, given their radically different theoretical propositions, Lenin's name is also cited in this context. However, so strange is this hypothecation, as Chris Brown has stressed, that we shall leave Lenin out of the argument here, as seems to me to be the case with contemporary English school advocates of world society.[23]

That a world society will be ethically cosmopolitan, or solidarist in English school terminology, can sometimes taken for granted, but there are writers who stress that this need not be the case. Certainly Barry Buzan's ambitious and wide-ranging re-formulation of the structure of English school theory makes the 'Kantian' label seem appropriate for only one possible, and not very probable, version of international society.[24] Even those who may not start from Buzan's radical re-write may still argue that a cosmopolitan interpretation of world society ought not to be seen as inevitable or even necessarily desirable.[25] This latter point, about the normatively problematic assumption of a cosmopolitan world society, is something that we shall look at briefly in this chapter and return to in more detail in Chapter 4.

Whilst this schematic framework for thinking about international relations has its problems, with the underdeveloped idea of world society being amongst the most significant in the light of the arguments about fundamental political transformations we briefly looked at in the Introduction, it does retain important benefits.[26] One of the most important of these is the methodological felxibility of such an approach. A key plank of the defence of the English school developed by Richard Little, for instance, is that it is able to draw on a variety of methodological approaches to understanding international relations, offering a forum and structure within which these different insights can be considered.[27] More specifically, Tim Dunne and others have pointed to the way in which the English school's methodology can, and should, be made explicitly constructivist.[28] This will offer surer methodological foundations to the approach than those existing in the work that established the idea of an English school in the 1960s and 1970s, and enable it to utilise the explanatory and critical tools that are available through making such a move.[29]

The efforts to develop constructivism more generally also point to the ways in which the kind of model roughed out by the English school is coming into the mainstream of international relations. The similarities between Alexander Wendt's tripartite classification of 'cultures of anarchy' into 'Hobbesian', 'Lockeian' and 'Kantian' modes bear striking similarities to the Hobbesian, Grotian and Kantian labels of the English school.[30] This is not, though, to say that we can simply adopt Wendt's approach. This is not simply because it, too, has problems – all efforts to theorise about a social phenomenon as complex as international relations will have problems.[31] More significant is Wendt's reliance on a symbolic interactionist sociological method that tends to restrict the kind of critical potential that the English school seeks to exploit, particularly through the idea of world society.[32] It is notable that Wendt's categories fail to escape the statist trap that the political geography literature considered in Chapter 2 is so critical of, and thus his schema struggles to encompass some of the ethical and normative debates that are central to our exploration of territorial borders.[33]

The normative agenda most closely associated with the English school is probably the tension between order and justice in international relations, and the connections between these two positions and the cosmopolitan and communitarian, or solidarist and pluralist, positions we have come across already. This tension manifests itself in international society in ways that are mirrored in policy discussions about humanitarian intervention in particular, and this has been a major theme of English school research in recent years, but which also have relevance to the war on terror.

The problem is easy to state, but fiendishly difficult to resolve. Indeed, it may well be irresolvable, which in part helps to explain the desire to explore seriously the idea of world society as a place in which resolution may be easier. Essentially, the idea(l) of Westphalian sovereignty brings with it as an inevitable corollary the rule of non-intervention. If a state, as part of the definition of what a state is, is to exert domestic supremacy over a specified and bordered segment of the planet's surface, and that the status of sovereignty requires the mutual recognition of that status between two or more states then each state must commit themselves to refrain from challenging that supremacy by trying to impose their will upon another. If, in addition to domestic supremacy, sovereignty includes a claim to be able to act autonomously on the international stage, then the requirement for non-intervention is reinforced further by the mutual requirement to respect the right of each state to reach autonomous decisions about how to conduct its foreign policy.[34]

Clearly, what constitutes intervention in the domestic affairs of another sovereign state is open to debate. Diplomatic pressure, trade preferences or restrictions, civil society connections, international media outlets and a great deal else could be said to influence the domestic politics of another state in some way, shape or form, whether intentionally or unintentionally. In order to avoid the *reductio ad absurdum* that beckons, there has emerged a more or less stable consensus that *coercive* and perhaps especially *militarily coercive* actions are what count as intervention.[35] This definition is problematic and controversial in a number of ways, not least because there are actions, like economic sanctions and the kind of structural adjustment programmes that are often a condition of International Monetary Fund or World Bank assistance, that are difficult to classify.[36] In the case of the latter in particular, it may be that the state seeking additional assistance could refuse to agree to the conditions, and forego the assistance, but that the consequences of such a course of action may be so economically catastrophic, and with attendant human costs in terms of spending on health, education and other socially desirable activities, as to make a 'No' almost unconscionable. To borrow metaphors from popular culture, this may not be holding a gun to the head of the state concerned, which would rob it of all meaningful agency and be an act of brute coercion, but it is to make it an offer that it cannot refuse.

As a result of these kinds of taxonomic difficulties, and attendant theoretical and conceptual debates about the nature of intervention and the difference between threats and offers and the like, the concept of intervention is a difficult one. However, it is one that international politics is saddled with as a result of the construction of sovereignty that dominates the subject. One rather minor potential benefit of the putative demise of the Westphalian system would be the sparing of academics from furthering agonising over this issue. Ethical questions about the extent to which domestic supremacy and international autonomy can be infringed upon are more germane to this argument, though, than efforts to refine, or abolish, the concept of intervention.

The defence of sovereignty and the non-intervention norm usually rests on the way in which states have been able to develop a functioning international society that delivers a degree of orderliness in international life. Despite the conflictual pressures generated first by the absence of over-arching authority that is a concomitant of sovereignty and secondly by the diversity of social, cultural, ethical and normative practices and schemas that exist in the world, the current pattern of international activity is reasonably orderly. The 'anarchical society' of states has been able to develop a widespread consensus about basic rules governing three key aspects of social life amongst states – rules on violence, rules on property and rules on promises and contracts. These are the fundamental bases without which no society can exist, whether one of human beings or political collectivities like states, and that their removal or destruction brings with it the peril of descent into an asocial or anti-social condition, best summarised by Thomas Hobbes' famous account of the state of nature – a warre of all against all.[37]

The story as usually told sees the origins of this society of states in early modern Europe. The 1648 Peace of Westphalia is portrayed as the crucial event that sees an anarchical society predicated on sovereignty triumph over hierarchical power structures, in which individuals like the Pope or Holy Roman Emperor, or, perhaps a better locution, institutions like the Papacy and the Holy Roman Empire, legitimately claim supranational political authority. The bitter, brutal and enormously destructive Thirty Years' War that ravaged much of central Europe in particular and involved all the major powers had been the final convulsion that had made territorially specific claims to sovereignty the only acceptable basis for political authority in Europe.[38] This system, with many teething problems and some significant amendments along the way, for example a move from absolute monarchs claiming divine right as the basis of sovereignty to a popular form in which sovereignty is seen to reside in the people, was globalised through European colonialism and, finally, de-colonisation.[39]

A global political system thus emerged for the first time and, despite the violence inflicted on the political authority structures of colonial peoples, it is one that enjoys very widespread acceptance. Even those groups unhappy with the current territorial borders of states often seek to change them to create new states for minority groups, or to bring together divided communities, rather than arguing for some sort of non-territorially bordered political space on non-sovereignty-based system of political authority. As Chris Brown points out, even those political leaders who resist ideas such as human rights on the grounds that they are Western and thus apparently inherently imperialistic are perfectly happy to subscribe to the equally Western and thus presumably also imperialistic idea of sovereignty, and to be among its most passionate defenders.[40]

This story may be just that – a significantly fictionalised account of historical events, with the Peace of Westphalia being particularly egregiously misrepresented – but it is a very powerful story.[41] Territorial borders play an important, if largely implicit, part in this scheme, because of their position as constitutive of what it means for a state to be a state and as essential in delimiting the extent of sovereign claims to authority. They are thus granted ethical significance because of the role that they play in creating order in these conditions of anarchy and cultural and ethical diversity.

Order and (in)justice in anarchy and diversity

The global international society of sovereign states that emerged after the Second World War, with large-scale de-colonisation creating tens of new states from previous colonial entities, is, according to the English school's historical account of the European international society, an unusual one.[42] This distinctiveness is in large part due to the degree of diversity of cultural and ethical traditions and practices that are present in international society. Compared to its European forebears, the post-1945 society of states lacks what Bull saw as the common civilisational traits that had helped provide social glue in previous eras.[43] The Christian inheritance common to Europe may have been violently schismatic during the reformation and the counter-reformation, with the Thirty Years' War as the apogee of this conflict, but it had created certain common ideas, notions and even values. The natural law tradition may have been fought over bitterly, especially in relation to the position of non-European peoples within it, but it did provide a framework for ethical debate.[44] Even the move to a positivist conception of law did not wholly eradicate this cultural heritage. Equally, the legacy of the Enlightenment and the sharing of a canon of political thought going back to the classical world reinforced a sense of relatedness amongst the European members of international society, and their settler outposts in North and South America, Australasia, Africa and Asia.

The globalisation of this international society may have seen some sort of consensus about the doctrine of sovereignty, but obviously not a consensus on this richer, more extensive heritage of social, political and ethical theory and practice. This, as pluralists in the English school stress heavily, has made particularly acute the problems of generating order and emphasised the need to protect the basis of order that does exist. The structure of order in the current international society is thus particularly fragile and perhaps more reliant than in the past on the formalities of international law.[45] This is not to say that states are any more likely to abide by international law than in the past, and the perennial problems associated with law that cannot be reliably and consistently enforced persist, especially in the face of a particularly extreme inequality in the distribution of power. However, the need for states to continue to portray their actions in terms that are cognisant with international law and to uphold a formal commitment to the legal rules of international society is particularly important. Given the difficulties of reaching the agreements that do exist and the need to rely on formalities in the absence of a less tangible, but probably more durable, sense of shared commitment to a common endeavour underpinned by values, efforts to shift the rules and practices of international society in dramatic ways are dangerous and misguided.

Efforts to assert such a sense of shared commitment to common values producing a consensus on the nature, purpose and direction of international society are better understood, on this view, either as acts of power or as examples of wishful thinking.[46] We may want to assert that the liberal version of the human rights claim is, logically and intellectually, irrefutable and that in any reasonable contest in which the force of the better argument will win out then we would all accept these sorts of claims. There are, of course, different versions of the liberal rights story, though, such as those associated with John Rawls, Brian Barry and Henry Shue, to name only a few possibilities.[47]

Equally, we can arrive at technically different sorts of cosmopolitan schemas that, in practice, would still significantly downgrade the role of sovereignty and treat territorial borders as ethically arbitrary. The form of discourse ethics associated with Jurgen Habermas in political theory and most rigorously argued for in international relations by Andrew Linklater is one such approach.[48] Richard Shapcott has argued elegantly for a cosmopolitan scheme that derives from the philosophical hermeneutics of Gadamer.[49]

For some, such as Nigel Dower, the 'source-story' for a cosmopolitan ethic ultimately is not all that important.[50] That very similar ethical schemes and normative propositions can be arrived at from a variety of philosophical starting points is possibly even a sign of the strength of these kinds of claims and that to rest the validity of cosmopolitanism on resolving the disputes between these source stories in order to prove the philosophical superiority of one or other of them is unnecessary. That so many good arguments can be put forward for ethical universalism is what matters, and what generates the normative imperative to move the politics of the world in a cosmopolitan direction. Peter Jones offers a somewhat different argument, although to similar effect, in his analysis of human rights as being best understood as a way to resolve differences between more specific ethical theories, particularly those arising from different cultural, religious or other similar sorts of contexts, rather than as an alternative to these that can only succeed by replacing them.[51]

However, of course, politics is not determined by the force of the better argument alone. Indeed, some pluralists may want to be solidarists – the position some argue Hedley Bull adopted – but they cannot allow that pure argument can provide a basis for overriding what they see as the harsh 'realities' of the Westphalian system.[52] Even appealing to the mass of widely signed, if usually somewhat less widely ratified, international conventions, declarations, covenants and treaties on human rights as evidence of a consensus amongst states in favour of such rights does not satisfy pluralists. They point instead to the declaratory nature of many of these instruments, and to the way in which alongside the grand language of universalism are usually to be found unqualified commitments to the principles of sovereignty, non-intervention and territorial integrity, irrespective of the intellectual inconsistency that this generates. Perhaps only in Europe, and then maybe only in its central and western parts, is there a genuine, institutionally entrenched and effectively enforceable human rights regime.[53]

Appeals to ethical universals are especially foolhardy on this view, because they threaten to generate conflicts over issues that are amongst the least likely to be resolved and the most likely to generate hostility and mistrust. In this, if nothing else, there is a connection to territorial borders which, as Barbara Walter argues, provide the source for similarly intractable and irresolvable conflicts.[54] The solidarist advocates of, for example, a limited right to humanitarian intervention are thus playing with fire. Not only are they seeking to open the can of worms that is the debate over ethical universality on the basis of human rights, the practical implications of humanitarian intervention have also often involved the creation of new states, or state-like entities, establishing border disputes that could run for decades. Whether it be the autonomous Kurdish zone of northern Iraq, the two post-Dayton entities of Bosnia or the NATO protectorate of Kosovo, humanitarian intervention has created border disputes.

From a pluralist perspective, a general hostility to terrorists may be easier to generate, perhaps in a similar way to the global outlawing of piracy,[55] but, of course, working out who is a terrorist is a much more controversial matter. This is not to make the oft-repeated, but still logically flawed, claim that 'one man's terrorist is another man's freedom fighter' or to argue that the ends justify the means, especially if those fighting for a good cause face overwhelming military odds. School and theatre sieges and suicide bombings expressly aimed at maximising civilian casualties are, in my view, beyond meaningful ethical defence, but it is to acknowledge the force of the point that the 'war on terror' usually favours the established political authorities, irrespective of the defensibility of their claim to authority, because of the way that the terrorism targeted by such a war is usually assumed to be the terrorism of non-state actors. 'State-sponsored terror' is a label that has currency in international relations and political debate more widely, but it is one that advocates of the war on terror, especially in government circles, have generally been reluctant to admit to the debate, save in the case of supposedly 'rogue states'.

This kind of critique of cosmopolitan claims essentially rests on the notion that there is an insufficient level of commonality in the value systems and ethical ideas in the world to bear the weight of controversial, expensive and violent action that overrides the Westphalian notion of sovereignty. It does not really matter whether the basis of universal claims are philosophical in origin or more pragmatic and rooted in treaties, declarations and the like. Territorial borders are seen as a blockage to the development of this kind of commonality and it is therefore not altogether surprising that it is to border-negating activities that cosmopolitans often look in their search for the emergence of a strong enough universal ethical framework. Cosmopolitanism is not just about somewhat idealistic projects for a perfect, or at least substantially better, world: they are plugged into real and important changes taking place in international relations that offer an opportunity for change that is there for the taking, if we can use our ethical compass to give direction to a coherent normative project.[56] Thus globalisation and the purported emergence of global civil society may offer another way of more adequately framing humanitarian crises because it downplays the role of territorial borders that contribute so significantly to the present logjam. Empirical changes in the nature and structure of international relations may help a cosmopolitan ethic, and its associated normative project of a greater role for justice in international politics, come to fruition.

Globalisation and the contingency of territorial borders

The normative assault on the Westphalian system characteristically stems from the inequities and injustices of the current international order. Crudely, it might be summarised by the claim that the price that is paid for the order that international society is said to generate is far too high. In particular, re-orientating our ethical compass in order to recognise that it is human beings that are the site of moral agency, and not sovereign states, reinforces the idea that international society has become a 'global gangster' – the operatives of a kind of global protection racket for states that see huge numbers of human beings forced to lead lives characterised by poverty, disease, malnutrition, political repression, torture, warfare and a host of other privations.[57] A great many of these are preventable, making a defence of international society even more untenable.

The defence of territorial borders offered by the traditional pluralist position within the English school is predicated on their contribution to order. International society needs territorial borders as fences between states because they make sovereignty possible and without sovereignty international society would be unable to generate the rules on violence, property and agreement that are the minimum conditions of order. Without order then 'higher' ethical questions, like justice, would be meaningless, at least in terms of practical politics, and consequently order must be seen as a 'prior value' and of almost inestimable importance.[58] The further complication of the ethical diversity of human societies reinforces the need for order, given the lack of any substantive consensus on the nature of justice, and territorial borders play a useful role in marking off areas of the world where different ethical schemas operate, allowing for diversity within broad ethical traditions to reflect local interpretations, debates, social structures and situations. This division is somewhat crude and imperfect, but it is reasonably workable, and the costs of trying to radically restructure it are too high.

> The vast majority of states seem to regard inherited boundaries as, on balance, both advantageous and legitimate and thus as a basis of both order and justice in world politics.... There is thus a compelling common interest in supporting the current juridical norm. Existing borders express a rare international consensus that gets beyond culture, religion, language, and most other sociological divisions between people.... International boundaries provide...a universally recognizable standard to live by. It may not be just. It may not be equitable. But it has the enormous practical advantage of being determinate and predictable.[59]

This makes a defence of territorial borders contingent, though, as do the cosmopolitan critiques on the grounds of justice. For the defenders of a pluralist, order-centred account of international society territorial borders have ethical significance because of the way that they serve the needs of order. If another mechanism could be found to divide up ownership, to act as mechanisms for helping distinguish between aggression and self-defence (by asking who crossed the border first?), we could do away with territorial borders. This is very unlikely, in practical terms, but it is not theoretically inconceivable. The sense of the embedding of the Westphalian system as being so great as to make alternatives appear almost automatically fantastical or utopian may be considerable, and important, but as Chris Brown points out, the idea of seeing beyond the end of a familiar and long-standing political constellation is a challenge that has faced all those seeking to understand their political circumstances during periods of change.[60]

The ethics of Westphalian territorial borders are not set in stone. The social practices of bordering on the basis of territorial delimitation and the ascription of sovereignty cannot be taken for granted as being the only way of doing things. In particular, the argument of a traditional defence of international society has to be understood as making the ethics of borders contingent on their ability to generate the value of order. This has also to be considered in the light of other ethical claims, and the need to balance competing notions of the good in social practice. Cosmopolitan critics, as we have seen, argue that the privileging of the state that comes with a Westphalian conception of international politics costs far too much in terms of human misery and injustice. Exclusively territorial notions of jurisdiction, identity and political authority must be challenged and changed. This, too, produces an account of territorial borders that treats them as contingent.

For example, the ideal of world government has long been abandoned by cosmopolitans. The practical difficulties of globally authoritative political institutions are one objection – a world government just would not work – but, more importantly for our perspective, the fear of the possibility of world government as world tyranny produces an even more telling knock-out blow against the idea.[61] The division of political authority thus becomes imperative, and, potentially, territorial borders can have a role to play in this division. It may even be the case that territorially bordered states could persist, making strong claims to authority over the land within their borders. However, this would have to be subject to what we might call a 'global justice test'.

This test could take at least two forms, although thinking about two will illustrate the point about the ethical contingency of borders sufficiently clearly. The first form is to look at the extent of the ramifications of action taken by a political authority. David Held's notion of 'cosmopolitan democracy', for example, makes important use of this argument to suggest that we need to recognise that the implications of actions taken at present may extend far beyond the borders of states and have highly detrimental consequences for individuals who have no say whatsoever in the decision-making process. This is unjust. It stands as a well-established point of political ethics, particularly of a liberal kind, that those who are significantly affected by a decision taken by political authority ought to possess either, and ideally both, an effective means of having their views taken into account during the decision-making process, or an effective means of redress.[62] Environmentally damaging actions are probably the clearest example of this kind of action,[63] but not the only kind, with regulatory decisions over the activities of multi-national corporations also having consequences for those well beyond the territorial borders of the state that ostensibly hosts the company concerned.[64]

The argument is that if we are to take seriously the democratic idea of political accountability and that this rests on the ability of governed individuals to have a say against those who take decisions that affect them, then we have to develop new and effective democratic decision-making mechanisms. These must be able to hold states to account for policy decisions that affect non-citizens in important ways and to hold transnational actors to account in ways that are not inherently biased towards the interests of only a small proportion of those who may suffer the consequences of their actions. Generating political constituencies on the basis of those affected by a particular decision, alongside a host of reforms to international organisations to ensure fairer representation for non-state agents in international politics and a far more effective and powerful set of enforcement mechanisms, is Held's vision of a solution to this problem of global social, political and economic activity outstripping both the political capacity and the ethical defensibility of a Westphalian system.[65] Territorial borders may therefore be ethically defensible but this will become almost entirely contingent on the needs of cosmopolitan democratic justice in the circumstances with which one is dealing. If we are dealing with a problem that is contained almost entirely within the borders of a current state and we can have faith in the ability of that state to deal with the problem in a democratic and just way then there is no need for the involvement of other states, other individuals or international or regional regulatory bodies.[66]

Held's reconstruction of the operation of international politics cannot be faulted for ambition, and, as with any such project, it is easy to pick holes and raise objections, both on the grounds of the difficulty of shifting existing practice and overcoming the prejudices of states on the one hand, and of some of the potential pitfalls in the scheme as proposed. For example, in an age when the United States cannot be persuaded of the need for it to change its patterns of fossil fuel consumption in the face of overwhelming evidence of climate change, or to sign up to the ICC as a mechanism for addressing what are accepted by the United States as crimes against humanity, then expecting it to agree to cosmopolitan democracy requires a leap of faith of enormous proportions. Similarly, if decisions are to be taken on the basis of the will of those who are likely to be affected then will it become necessary to gain the consent of those whose land will be the site of battle before military actions can be undertaken? It is rather difficult, again, to see the United States agreeing to the idea that it should have consulted with and fully taken into account the views of the population of Iraq before the United States could have invaded in 2003.

Such criticism is not wholly fair, though, and certainly it is just as easy to point to absurdities and impossibilities in the Westphalian system – it is just that we have become so used to them that they no longer strike us as glaring or outrageous examples of idiotic institutional design or blatantly unjust mechanisms for arriving at decisions. Held's vision reminds us of the opportunity for change that is present in international politics, as, in their rather less ambitious ways, do the advocates of new mechanisms to deal with humanitarian crises or the threat of global terrorism. The desirability of the institutional and other practical elements of the proposed solutions, or, more realistically, improvements on current mechanisms, is an ethical decision in important ways. One of the things that ties humanitarian intervention, the war on terror and cosmopolitan democracy together is the way in which they treat territorial borders as contingent – on the state's willingness to properly respect the prior right of human beings in the first case, on the state's ability to combat terrorism in the second and on the nature of the issue and the justice of the state concerned in the third.

There is, of course, no guarantee of overlap between these three, with a state's willingness to support the United States in the war on terror, for example, potentially buying it considerable leeway on its human rights record. There is plausible evidence that states with very poor human rights records have been used by the United States, and potentially other Western powers, as places where terrorist suspects can be interrogated under torture. The practice of returning terrorism suspects to countries where they face a very real risk of torture is also becoming common. The use by Western intelligence agencies and governments of information extracted under torture is deeply morally troubling, particularly from a cosmopolitan perspective.[67]

This connects with the second element of a cosmopolitan 'global justice test' that we can usefully consider. A hypothetical defender of the use of any information, however obtained, that may enable us to head off a terrorist attack or some other form of violent outrage may cite the prime moral responsibility of a government to protect its own citizens. They may claim that it is the job – in fact, the moral obligation – of government to privilege the interests of those whom it governs and to grant them special status and consideration in decision-making, especially where security is concerned.[68] This may extend to treating non-citizens as less ethically significant as citizens, perhaps even denying non-citizens certain rights that cosmopolitans would regard as universal and fundamental should that enable the government to better protect the rights of citizens. It would thus be unethical of a government to ignore information that came into its possession, no matter what its provenance, that might result in the government missing an opportunity to protect the lives of its citizens. If this comes at the price of colluding in the abuse of the human rights, even to the point of torture, then that would be ethically defensible.[69]

This kind of ethical discrimination flies in the face of a cosmopolitan position, and, indeed, there are a great many cosmopolitans who would regard torture, for example, as always wrong, no matter what the circumstances.[70] A high price may indeed have to be paid in order to avoid appearing to condone torture, let alone actively colluding in it. Our hypothetical defender of the use of information gained through torture may continue to argue that this is to play with the lives of those whom a government is charged with defending, and that asking people to face unnecessary risk of death, injury and the destruction of property for a principled opposition to torture is to require a government to act in opposition to its obligation to protect citizens, and to privilege their interests over the interests of foreigners.

This argument has weight, even if we might well wish to argue that colluding in or condoning the use of torture is to carry it too far. The idea that governments should privilege their own citizens over 'foreigners' plays out in a number of areas, including some that attract a good deal of controversy. The export of military equipment, especially where this is to governments with a less than glowing record of respecting human rights, is one such instance. Major arms exporting states, like the United Kingdom, enjoy a regular debate over the ethics of this activity, with critics arguing that it is unethical to export military equipment to governments that may use that equipment for internal repression. Less directly, it can also be argued that it is unethical to offer such governments tacit support through military sales, or even that in colluding with such expenditure the UK government is indirectly diverting funds from more socially just areas of expenditure, like education or political reform. Defenders of arms exports will generally cite the UN Charter right of all states to self-defence, regardless of their domestic politics, and may also point to the importance of sales of defence equipment (the government and industry euphemism for arms) to providing economies of scale that enable UK forces to be equipped with the best possible military equipment at more reasonable cost, reducing the burden on the tax payer. Finally, but commonly, they may highlight the number of jobs that the sector sustains in the United Kingdom.

This, too, is to make a claim about the differential ethical obligations that exist between different groups and how this works itself out in public policy. The military benefits to UK forces, the boost to the UK economy as a whole and the benefit to UK citizens of good jobs must be placed in the balance alongside any support for or benefit to repressive regimes. It is also, implicitly, to deploy an argument about the ethical standing of different kinds of actions rooted in socially constructed ideas of what is and what is not ethically defensible. It is important to note that these ideas are not fixed and, indeed, change quite dramatically over time. In this instance, arms sales are seen as falling very close to the line, attracting controversy. However, other actions that could, in theory, be defended on similar grounds of economic benefits are regarded as abhorrent. As Ken Booth points out with characteristic pithiness, those who defend the sales of arms on the basis of jobs and on the grounds that 'if we don't sell them, someone else will' do not apply the same logic to child pornography.[71]

Indeed, the development of prohibition regimes in international politics has encompassed a range of activities that were once state policy but which would now be regarded as abhorrent, and any state involving itself in such activities would seek to keep it very quiet indeed. So, for example, state-sponsored narcotics trading, as with the Opium Wars waged by the British against China in the nineteenth century to guarantee British opium dealers access to Chinese markets, is now condemned. So too is state-sponsored piracy, again marking a departure from the policy of the United Kingdom, and others, in the seventeenth century when figures such as Francis Drake and Walter Raleigh became heroes on the basis of what would today be seen as criminal activity. Perhaps the most striking shift is the now universal moral opprobrium heaped upon slavery – which, a short two hundred years ago, was widely seen in Europe and its settler colonies as morally acceptable, if not actually biblically authorised, and certainly economically essential. Where slavery, or indentured labour schemes that effectively amount to slavery, still persists it has been driven more or less underground and would find very few willing advocates.

Whilst social practices have moved away from condoning to condemning these activities, and contemporary debates have the potential to add new items to the 'condemned' list, privileging the interests of fellow nationals remains generally acceptable. The need to create a category, or categories, of those who possess rights, even if only additional rights, and to whom we owe special duties as a result of some kind of connection above and beyond any shared sense of being human is an enduring trait.[72] Doing this on the basis of citizenship – a formal connection to a territorially bordered place – is a particularly powerful mechanism for deciding who is in, and who is out; who counts, and for how much, if at all.[73]

Membership of the state thus brings with it what we might usefully label rights and duties of special beneficence, particularly in relation to what governments ought to do when judging how to balance the competing demands, needs and interests of those 'at home' against those 'abroad'.[74] Our global justice test does not produce a simple equality of rights, even if there are some rights that we may wish to see accorded to all, such as freedom from torture. The idea of duty is perhaps especially important here, because it asks the important cosmopolitan question of who has responsibility to act in the face of cosmopolitan ethical demands. In the absence of world government and the presence of some form of division, or bordering, of political authority there will almost always be someone, or some political entity, that has more of an obligation to respond to injustice. There are very few examples, perhaps only one that is very well known, of arguments for a global equality of responsibility for injustice and a universal duty to take action: Peter Singer's justly famous argument, on utilitarian grounds, in 'Famine, Affluence and Morality'.[75]

The details of Singer's argument are not terribly important here, interesting and thought-provoking though they remain more than 30 years after they were first promulgated. What is more striking is that it is difficult to think of another major cosmopolitan ethical theorist who has followed the lead Singer offered and attempted to make an argument for a universal and equal responsibility for addressing injustice and inequality. Singer's brand of utilitarianism is perhaps especially well suited to offering such an argument, but it is notable that liberals who make a great deal of room for rights in their theory nevertheless almost always have to go out of their way to offer an explanation for the ethical need to differentiate between those close to us and those further away. Sometimes this is done on the basis that such distinctions can contribute to the overall attainment of justice, but on others it recognises the power of identity and other kinds of attachments that people share, something that Chris Brown argues emphasises the need for political theory in this area to avoid being reduced to moral theory.[76] There is a need for our ethical test to include a mechanism for recognising the idea of rights and duties of special beneficence in our conception of a more just world order.

This bordering of ethical responsibility does not have to be territorial, of course, and in this instance it may well be that a territorial notion comes fairly low down the list of ways of identifying groups to whom we owe something over and above any universal ethical connections our form of cosmopolitanism requires us to recognise. Family, friends and others to whom we have powerful emotional attachments are the most obvious instances. It would be a very curious ethical theory indeed that, for example, condemned the man who saved his wife and children from a burning building before turning his attentions to any other occupants, even if he might possibly have saved more people in total had he left his family to burn to death.

Owing rights and duties of special beneficence to fellow citizens, the vast majority of whom we will have no personal knowledge of at all, is a bigger stretch, though. The ideas of patriotism, of ties resulting from a shared history, culture or sense of identity tied up in some way with the state are the grounds to which appeals are typically made.[77] Nationalism is obviously central to the way that this is cashed out in the contemporary world,[78] although as advocates of changes stemming from globalisation would be keen to point out, this kind of group-based 'we-feeling' is diversifying away from the state to include other kinds of group identities that deserve recognition for their ethical significance.[79] Territorial borders thus play a role in this kind of theory because of the way they delimit the extent of the state and, for the most part, the geographical distribution of the vast majority of citizens, as they will live within those borders. However, this is potentially just coincidental, and certainly grants territorial borders no particular ethical significance of their own on an automatic basis. Citizenship need not be territorially bounded or the only way of establishing ethically significant relationships to political authority. The place where one lives may be as ethically arbitrary as the size of one's feet or the colour of one's eyes.

Again, the ethical significance of territorial borders would seem to be contingent upon their serving some higher ethical duty or obligation, in this case some meaningful notion of national interest based on some substantive conception of shared communal membership able to provide good grounds for discriminating between 'us' and 'them'. Even in cases where people may appeal to the idea of specific locations as being of vital significance to their identity, it is to a particular place, not to the lines around it, that people are appealing. Efforts to exert exclusive control over such places may generate territorial borders, and may also generate a great many problems should such a site have significance for multiple identities. An example here would be the Temple Mount in Jerusalem, and the disputes between Jews and Muslims over control and access. Indeed the roughly one square kilometre that encompasses the whole of the old city of

Jerusalem, holy to three major religions, presents a number of fascinating and contentious border issues that extend well beyond the debate over the extent of Israel's sovereignty and the sovereignty of a putative Palestinian state as part of a two-state solution.[80] Justice in an instance such as this is very unlikely to be served by drawing a line and declaring the land on one side of it to belong exclusively to one state and that on the other side to belong exclusively to a different state.[81] This may well be what happens, but pragmatic political realities, including the relative power of the two sides, are likely to be seen as being at the root of such an outcome, rather than a feeling that it represents the most just possible solution to the problem.

The idea of using a notion such as rights and duties of special beneficence has many attractions, then, in thinking about how we respond to the pressures for a more ethically cosmopolitan view of the world.[82] It seems, too, to be in tune to some extent with the kinds of policy debates that have arisen, in which the responsibility to respond to humanitarian and other kinds of crises is typically ascribed to one group of states or a regional organisation. In debates about how to respond to the collapse of Yugoslavia, for example, the idea was very prominent that this was a European problem, and that it was for the European states, working through the EU, to take the lead.[83] Some former colonial powers also appear to believe that they have an enduring responsibility for their former colonies, with, for example, the United Kingdom offering assistance to Sierra Leone during the depths of its political crisis in 1999–2000.[84] Where a duty of beneficence ends and neo-colonialism starts can be controversial, though. There has been widespread questioning of the motives of the French government's involvement in some Francophone countries in Africa, with the example of Operation Turquoise in Rwanda being a prime example.[85]

Nevertheless, whatever the merits, or otherwise, of particular operations or policies, the idea of there being groups to whom 'we' owe something extra is a commonplace. The rhetoric of the war on terror, especially in the United States, has made great play of the idea of 'freedom-loving peoples', whom the United States is seeking to support in their aspiration to freedom, especially where they share a notion of freedom that emphasises individual rights and a liberal democratic and capitalist political-economic system.[86] Whilst we might balk at the rhetorical flourishes – 'freedom loving peoples', 'axis of evil' – the 'war on terror' (another such flourish) has seen US policy move in the direction of emphasising the contingency of the status of territorial borders through the mechanism of rights and duties of special beneficence – there are those to whom the United States owes something over and above any universal minimum. Put crudely, as George W. Bush did indeed put it immediately after 9/11, 'You're either with us or you are with the terrorists', with the clear implication that those 'with the terrorists' would be likely to find life being made very uncomfortable indeed.[87]

When limited to the level of the state, these kinds of arguments are not necessarily incompatible with an English school under-standing of international society. It is perfectly possible to imagine an international society of states in which those states whom 'we' are 'against', or to whom we deny ethical equivalence, are in a tiny minority. It is even possible to imagine a society of states in which there is no need for any such differentiation at all, because some genuinely consensual and universal ethical ideas have been, to all intents and purposes, attained. Such an international society would be far more solidarist than the one Hedley Bull described in the 1970s and 1980s, or that Robert Jackson describes currently.[88] It would be an international society in which states had been able to agree on a much wider range of ethical propositions and had inter-nalised those values and come to recognise a common good in the general suppression of activities that rely for their justification on culturally specific bases or which are inherently discriminatory on grounds that lack rational plausibility or general persuasiveness, like race or gender or religious faith or sexual orientation.[89] Such, at least, would be the kinds of bases that liberals would like to appeal to, and it is on a broadly liberal conception of the state that so much of this discussion has been based. The idea of the state as, to borrow from Rawls, 'a co-operative venture for mutual advantage' helps to produce the arguments for the contingency of territorial borders that we have considered. A solidarist international society of states would also seem to be most plausibly based on such a liberal notion, too, as it would enable what the English school regards as ethically progres-sive claims about human rights and universality to be advanced without requiring a fundamental shift in the current basis of order through territorial sovereignty.[90]

Such a system would also easily be able to accommodate variations on the liberal theme, as states are able to do at present in areas such as capital punishment, established religions, electoral systems and the presence of a monarchy. The level of ethical consensus characteristic of a solidarist international society may also enable it to accommodate, without too much strain, some of the forms of political allegiance and authority that are characteristic of the liberal accounts of globalisation that we have briefly considered. Supranational political bodies, with the EU the prime example, can use ideas such as a 'pooling' of sovereignty to fudge the partial break with a strict Westphalian conception that such an organisation represents. The operation of an effective European Court of Human Rights can also be fitted into the system because of the strength of the liberal consensus in Europe. The global economic regulatory roles played by an international organisation like the WTO and even by some private institutions, like the major credit rating agencies, also stretches, but does not break, the elasticity of a solidarist international society. Limited rights to humanitarian intervention and, somewhat less easily, perhaps, rights to preventative military action against terrorism may also be accommodated with revisions to, rather than revolution in, the structure of international society. A widespread role for non-governmental organisations (NGOs) operating internationally as well as nationally on key issues of global concern, like human rights, environmental change, economic development and crisis prevention, is another feature of contemporary international politics that a liberal ethical consensus would be likely to see extended further. In international relations terms, the number and diversity of actors involved in various regimes would be likely to increase, alongside the scope and authority of those regimes. The formal claims to sovereignty on the part of states would persist, but their ability to act autonomously would decline in the face of this enmeshment in an increasingly powerful web of transnational ties. The appeal to the purported legacy of Westphalia in such a system would become more and more rhetorical, even if this kind of model is well short of a full-blown cosmopolitan democracy.

This kind of liberal vision mixes elements of the English school ideal-types of international and world society, shifting the balance away from the international system understood in realist terms of violence, conflict and insecurity, where the balance of power is the dominant institution. It makes more explicit the ethical contingency of territorial borders and attempts to accommodate the kind of border-negating activity of globalisation whilst not abandoning entirely the basis of order in a territorially bordered sovereign states system. Nevertheless, neither this kind of cosmopolitanism nor the order-focused, pluralist alternative generally seen as the other position available within the English school can offer an account of territorial borders that grants them inherent ethical significance. If we are coming at this issue from a liberal perspective, then we appear compelled to reach a conclusion about territorial borders that sees them as possessing ethical significance purely because they may, in certain circumstances, provide a means to an end.

This kind of effort to encompass globalisation within English school theory, whereby the category of 'world society' is stretched to include a mixed system whereby an international society of states operates alongside and intermingled with the growing importance of non-state actors, non-statist political, economic and societal formations and networks, has been challenged by Buzan's re-working of English school theory.[91] His argument is sophisticated, complex and rigorous and makes a powerful case for maintaining an analytical distinction between international society, of states, and world society, populated by non-state actors. The 'world society as international society plus' position, roughed out above, argues Buzan, aims to incorporate so much into the 'world society' category as to make it analytically unworkable.

Exploring these categories separately enables a much clearer analysis to emerge from the different social processes that each involves, produces a clearer picture of the complementarities and conflicts that exist across the categories and enables a wide-ranging re-assessment of issues such as the pluralist–solidarist debate. It also enables a wider range of geographical scales to be included, particularly regionalism. Buzan argues that this avoids one of the pitfalls associated with the extant version of 'world society' which is to associate world society with ethical cosmopolitanism. This is helpful to the argument here, adding to support for Buzan's case on the basis of its analytical persuasiveness. However, Buzan's schema lacks an alternative normative agenda of its own, which is one of the attractive things about the efforts by English school solidarists to push their version of 'world society'. Whilst Buzan sees solidarism as most likely to appear amongst states, he divorces solidarism from ethical cosmopolitanism, seeing it instead as more of a settled consensus around a set of shared values, which need not be cosmopolitan. Thus pluralism, as typically understood by the English school in terms of ethical diversity, could itself be a form of solidarism if there is a settled consensus that such diversity is desirable and effective rules are widely shared for enabling co-existence.[92] Apart from being somewhat confusing, at least at first, or even second, sight, as Buzan himself acknowledges, this normative neutrality is something of a weakness, at least to my eyes.

There are those, in the United States, notably, who regard Buzan's re-working as commendable because of the way it brings the English school closer to the mainstream social scientific tradition that is dominant there, part of which is a deep-rooted suspicion of normative theory.[93] However, the willingness to present normative arguments in defence of the ethics of a particular construction of international society is one of the defining features of English school theory, and whilst Buzan's re-working certainly does not preclude this, indeed may well help in strengthening those arguments, it does not point terribly clearly in any direction at present.

Sidestepping the ethics of territorial borders

The main problem with both the traditional, conservative, pluralist approach and the liberal-based efforts to promulgate a powerful cosmopolitan ethic is that they both sidestep the question of the ethics of territorial borders. These profoundly important features of political life become the by-products of statehood, uninteresting in and of themselves and existing solely in order to mark the end of one claim to exclusive authority and the beginning of another. The lines on the map remain very little more than lines on the map in terms of the conceptual exploration that they warrant.

From the discussion in Chapter 2 we can see that this is unsatisfactory for all the kinds of reasons that critical geopolitics and political geography has been arguing for. In trying to answer some important normative and ethical questions about the nature of international society, such as how states as possessors of some degree of agency and actorly quality create and sustain aspects of social life and what this means for advocacy of the ethical primacy of human beings as agents, the kinds of debates between pluralists and solidarists on the issues of international justice have overlooked the border question.

The idea of rights and duties of special beneficence has proven useful as a way to recognise the importance of state-based forms of political authority and of identity whilst opening room for non-state forms. However, this only works up to a point. In particular, whilst the idea enables us to recognise the role of non-state based forms of community in establishing ethical ties that people can reasonably be expected to take into account, it is limited by an overarching and ultimately dominant cosmopolitan reading of the basis of human ethical standing. This is most easily accommodated if a strong reading of the globalisation hypothesis is accepted and it is assumed that the kinds of non-state political actors and forms are increasingly taking on a level of importance that will shortly equal or surpass that of the state. This will enable the Westphalian privileging of the state to be done away with, at least on a *de facto* basis. As a result, the state can be seen, as with other kinds of co-operative ventures for mutual advantage, which might well include firms, NGOs and even looser types of transnational ties such as those associated with diasporas, as a means to an end of approximating a notion of a good human life that enjoys general, and genuine, consensus. We may want, in the light of Buzan's critique, to see this as more expressly normative, and less the result of arguments about the direction of globalisation, but this analytical claim does not lead to a clear and specific normative or ethical defence of pluralism as ethical diversity.

The cosmopolitan normative proposition draws on both empirical claims about change in international politics – led by the economic sector and concentrated in certain parts of the world, particularly the advanced, industrialised world – and on a broad liberal tradition of ethical and political thinking which has echoes in public political debate. It produces a model that may even be approximated within the EU. In offering a multi-layered, pluralistic version of a global world it stands apart from the state-centrism of Westphalia and is thus able to tap into the discontent with the injustices of the Westphalian system that we have considered, without falling into similar, if differently shaped, pitfalls that might arise in offering an alternative predicated on a single ontologically prioritised political formation.

In comparison to a strongly Westphalian approach stressing the need for order in conditions of structural anarchy and widespread ethical diversity the cosmopolitan, globalised (or at least partially globalised) multi-layered alternative looks to be ethically progressive and intellectually more insightful. The downgrading of territorial borders is an inescapable part of this kind of proposal, driven by both the logics of the empirical claims about the nature and extent of globalisation, especially as that is driven by a neo-liberal notion of economic systems, and by the broadly liberal cosmopolitan ethical consensus. This kind of approach even has echoes in public policy debates. In relation to the Iraq War in 2003, Tony Blair led the British government in putting forward a view of the problems that Iraq represented and also the opportunities that he saw for a post-Saddam Iraq to be re-integrated into this kind of liberal order. Joining together globalisation with an argument about the changing security challenges represented by transnational terrorism and the ethical imperatives of human rights has created an idea of Iraq as potentially in the vanguard of taking this kind of political model to the Middle East. Blair seems to see this operating effectively in the North-Atlantic area and to work on the assumption that regional circumstances, cultural morés and potential religious objections will either be overcome or can be accommodated within this approach.[94]

Territorial borders thus seem to effectively disappear as serious political questions, at least in terms of having to develop some sort of political theory to understand them or having to make space for them normatively. Where useful, they can endure, mainly in dividing up those parts of political authority that continue to be territorialised. Where harmful or just plain irrelevant, then they can be set aside as different mechanisms are found for working out questions of authority. Unfortunately, this neglects the enduring role that territorial borders play in conflict and violence in international relations in a large number of cases. Casting this as some sort of antediluvian throwback to a fast-disappearing Westphalian era is one way out of this but it relies on a teleological reading of history or a strong faith in the ability of humans to learn from their mistakes and not make them again. Neither of these tendencies are unknown in the liberal tradition, but they ought not to be taken for granted. The iterative process whereby Kant suggests perpetual peace will be created offers a connection to the Kantian tradition in the English school.[95]

Attaching territorial borders rigidly to the state, though, points to the way in which the traditional pluralist version of the English school, and those English school and other cosmopolitans looking to some form of world society, fall foul of the 'territorial trap', or at least a version of it.[96] The key failure here is to assume a too-strong link between territorial borders and sovereignty and thus make an assumption that non-state-based political forms must in some fundamental sense be de-territorialised. This may be true in some cases, such as capital markets, which do seem to operate in ways that are almost entirely disconnected from a conventional geography of politics, but it is not necessarily true of most of the other features of world society. Transnational social movements may appeal to universal ideals such as human rights and environmental sustainability or even more abstract notions such as justice, but in as much as these are usually discussed in relation to human beings as the principal referent then they cannot be effectively understood outside of social context and beyond the ways in which they are socially constructed. Extending the inclusiveness of these concepts, especially environmental thinking, to include all living things is one way in which a genuinely global conception, divorced from a primarily human social scale, can be achieved, but it is one that has found few adherents beyond a small number of 'deep green' environmental theorists.[97]

Bordering, often on the basis of territory, instead needs to be understood and explored as a social practice that stands separate to the creation of sovereign states. The sedimentation or reification of territorial borders into the sovereign state model has blinded international political theory to this important insight and produced the kind of impoverished, strictly contingent reading of the ethics of territorial borders that we have considered in this chapter. Bringing into play the insights of political geography to augment and extend the ways in which international political theory has so powerfully pushed forward ethical and normative questions in international relations in the last 15 years can enable a richer and deeper account of the ethics of territorial borders that avoids contingent conclusions.

This has benefits beyond simply making a contribution to the international political theoretical debate, whether this is cast in English school terms or not. This has been a useful way to approach these problems and has helped to frame the mainly liberal defences of cosmopolitan ethics that we have considered, too, but the critique applies with almost equal force to other kinds of theoretical and normative constructions of territorial borders common in international relations in particular. The connection between nationalism and the kind of order-based pluralist defence of borders discussed in English school terms above is well entrenched in the conduct of international relations via the hugely powerful connection between nationalism and statehood through the post-colonial triumph of national self-determination as the legitimate basis for statehood. In practice, of course, this has been tightly constrained in order to prevent secession, irredentism and other disorder inducing claims being granted much house-room, further reinforcing the territorial borders–statehood–international order logic of pluralism.[98]

It is therefore necessary to find a way in which the pieces of the jigsaw that have been assembled can be put together in such a way that the focus shifts more closely to territorial borders in and of themselves, rather than seeing them rather too simply as being just the lines on the map that delimit to extent of sovereign statehood, whereby it is the concept of sovereignty and the institution of the state that deserve all the ethical scrutiny. Clearly it would be absurd to suggest that the ethics of territorial borders can or should supplant the ethics of sovereignty or the ethics of the state, but neither is it a good idea to automatically subsume the ethics of territorial borders into these other fields. Looking at territorial borders as social practices that are connected to but not exhausted by the practices of the state and of sovereignty opens some critical perspective upon them, connects territorial borders to other kinds of borders and boundaries in social practice and enables us to think more clearly about whether or not territorial borders are ethically defensible in and of themselves, rather than as some instrumental adjunct of something else.

4
Valuing Borders (and Bordering Values?)

Introduction

Seeing territorial borders as part of a cosmopolitan ethic within an understanding of the nature of change in international politics that stresses a broadly liberal theory of the state and a liberal-capitalist mode of globalisation has major problems. So too does trying to restrict the role of territorial borders to being the fences of the international system, dividing what is regarded as the far more conceptually interesting and rich notion of sovereignty. This renders borders as a necessary and highly determined by-product of the claim to exclusive domestic authority and international autonomy. The ethical contingency of borders in both cases is the problem here.

However, in this chapter we move on to look at how the pluralist approach that was found wanting in Chapter 3 does have the potential to offer an account of the ethics of territorial borders that avoids, or at least very greatly weakens, the claim to strictly contingent ethical standing for territorial borders and enables some of the insights into globalisation coming from the cosmopolitans to be taken on board, and some of the ethical opportunities, too. This approach moves the emphasis in explanations of territorial borders away from sovereignty and instead sees the role of ethical diversity on a global scale as being more important. This involves an account of the relationship between sovereignty and ethical diversity that sees diversity as being prior to sovereignty, with sovereignty as an imperfect and temporary mechanism to address the political challenges diversity presents. This can still leave sovereignty as the primary constitutive norm or institution of international society, but breaks the assumption of most pluralist thinking, not just within the English school, but thinking more generally about the issue of ethical diversity, that the international political significance of diversity stems from the creation of a sovereign state system.

Instead, this chapter shall try to argue for a more complex and symbiotic relationship between these two that gives us purchase on how territorial borders are more complicated than sovereignty generally allows and that they play an important role in and of themselves in setting the basis for toleration of ethical diversity that reflects the ethical desirability of such diversity. This chapter, and the book as a whole, is thus at odds with cosmopolitan ethics, at least as such ethics have been portrayed so far, and also rejects the static and unconvincing account of pluralism offered by most English school pluralists in particular.

In terms of the political circumstances that we have been considering throughout – aspects of globalisation, ideas of humanitarian intervention and the idea of a post-9/11 global war on terror – the approach mapped out here offers some critical insights into the way that these can be seen as holding out hope for a more universalist form of international, or global, politics that seeks to bring people closer together in their ideas about how the world is, and, more importantly here, should be organised. The kind of universalism developed is not, though, of a liberal kind that rests on some sort of story, or set of stories, about the commonality of human individuals. Instead, it rests on a commonality of community membership, on the need for people to belong in order to possess a sense of identity that must, in some ways, require them to be able to distinguish themselves from others. This line of argument, especially in relation to political identity, draws on a more civic-republican tradition of thought and, in particular, owes some important debt to the political theory of Hannah Arendt, a figure who has made relatively little impact on international relations to date.[1] Political identity receives the most attention here because it is the most politically significant, if that is not wholly tautological, and also because it is political identity that plays such a central role in the reification of territorial borders that has hamstrung international political theory's engagement with the ethics of borders. This produces a limited defence of the ethical significance of territorial borders on the basis of their importance to the manifestation and maintenance of diversity in international politics, the ethical desirability of such diversity and the need to create a system whereby such diversity can find ways of co-existing on the basis of toleration.

This appeal to a political ethic of toleration will result in some critical engagement with the idea of toleration, too, as this is often portrayed as being an almost quintessentially liberal virtue, thus potentially pitching us back into the same sort of unsatisfactory liberal accounts of territorial borders we have just attempted to escape from.[2] However, the version of toleration that the chapter develops is not a straightforwardly liberal one, and again links up with the kind of political theory associated with Arendt in, hopefully, productive ways. One of the most difficult challenges facing any appeal to toleration is to be able to define what is intolerable and the chapter aims to address this as, in part, a response to the challenge of abandoning a more straightforward, liberal cosmopolitanism by instead generating some kind of alternative account of an ethical minimum for international politics, especially as it struggles to deal with issues of violence and terrorism, human rights abuses and deprivation, globalisation and the marginalisation of some people, especially the poor, that goes along with it.

The first part of the chapter thus looks at the idea of toleration in some detail in order to explain how it is that a fairly straightforward, liberal approach to toleration is unsatisfactory, particularly as we attempt to take it from within the state, where two of the founders of the liberal idea of toleration we shall consider, Locke and J. S. Mill, located it, to the international system. The dangers of the domestic analogy, well known in international relations, are a part of the problem here but the greater scope and extent of ethical diversity at the global level also highlights and exacerbates some of the problems with the approach that are normally contained by restricting toleration to being within the state.

The chapter then moves on to a revised notion of toleration, drawing on Hannah Arendt's political thought in some important ways, to offer a different reading of toleration that, the argument claims, is far better suited to international relations, even under conditions of globalisation. In important measure, this is because of the way that we regain critical and ethical perspective on and insight into the social practice that is the territorial border, showing that it can have ethical value in and of itself. This is not to claim that all the territorial borders of the world are ethically defensible, or that the political map of the world must remain frozen as it currently is. Some territorial borders may not be ethically defensible and the defensibility of others may change over time and in response to circumstances. However, these are matters for case-by-case evaluation, rather than abstract, theoretical determination. More important is simply to make the case that we can, and should, investigate territorial borders in ethically informed ways, and not just treat them as the lines on the map or in the sand, that are uninteresting in and of themselves, save in the practical implications of their location, with even that being determined primarily by the distribution of other political questions and forces.

Toleration, territorial borders and the burden of diversity

Toleration is demanding. It require us '...to practice tolerance even when it is troublesome and painful to do so'.[3] Toleration is about accepting the validity of things that we find distasteful, even things we find morally abhorrent.[4] Toleration is thus often linked with liberty and a liberal view of politics. However, this may not be a wholly satisfactory position.

Toleration as a specifically liberal virtue is a common idea, with some useful parallels to the kind of discussions present in the English school that we looked at in Chapter 3. Indeed, Robert Jackson specifically identifies his version of pluralism with a liberal 'forbearance and toleration'.[5] John Locke and J. S. Mill offer the principal sources for a liberal approach to toleration. Elements of both are discernible in the debates about a pluralist need to tolerate ethical diversity in the name of order, and a more cosmopolitan argument about toleration of different ways in which political institutions and practices may operate in response to local conditions and circumstances. Locke's position offers perhaps the most immediately obvious parallel to international relations, in this instance the argument for toleration to maintain order in the face of diversity, and it is with this argument that we shall start.

Locke's discussion of toleration takes place against a backdrop of religious questions and the diversity of religious faith. Then, as now, religious issues appeared to present some of the most difficult problems in political life, given the ways in which religious doctrine and faith could be appealed to in defence of acts of violence, repression, discrimination and exclusion. In particular, religion presents liberalism with major problems because of the role of faith in establishing the authority of religious tenets and beliefs. Certainly to twenty-first-century eyes, the liberal appeal to the power of reason, to the secularisation of knowledge and the spotlighting of the sovereign, rational individual as the centrepiece of political thinking offers little scope for religious faith as a basis for politically valid knowledge. This, of course, is to make an appeal to the idea of a public/private divide, in which matters which are not easily contained within a framework of rational individualism or seen as an unavoidable part of the creation of a polity are enclosed within the private realm, de-politicised and taken out of the public realm in so far as that is possible.[6] Thus, to take a simple example, in a liberal political system the religious faith of political leaders is, or ought to be, primarily a private matter. As well as it being unreasonable to discriminate against a potential leader on the grounds of their belief it is also unreasonable for them to take public, political decisions on the basis of their faith. Appeals to religious rhetoric and claims to be upholding religiously inspired values are not, of course, unknown in the politics of liberal states, even in states where there is a constitutionally entrenched separation of church and state. For example, in France, opponents of EU enlargement to include Turkey appeal to the idea of the EU as a 'Christian club'.[7] In the United States, religious revivalism and the power of Christian political movements, generally on the conservative right, have made appeals to Christian values almost *de rigeur* for successive presidents over the last 20 years.[8]

The public/private divide has, of course, been the subject of serious critique for a long time. Feminist political theorists have made a major impact here, pointing up the way in which the gendering of women discriminates against their involvement in the public, political realm by creating a notion of femininity that downplays the political virtues and ascribes to women roles that are focused on the home, the epitome of the private realm. In international relations, this critique has been repeated, with major work showing how what are usually portrayed as central issues in international relations – war and security – have been discussed in ways that exclude or downgrade women. This highlights how it is that our idea of 'international relations' often repeats the same kind of gendered discourse and exclusionary social practice that occurs in 'domestic' politics, too.[9]

Locke's argument is hardly the place to expect a sophisticated discussion of the gender aspects of the problems of the public/private divide, but his argument for toleration does offer an interesting example of how this divide can generate what, at least on the face of it, are appealing political consequences that continue to attract support to this day. Locke advocates religious toleration because he believes that coercing genuine faith is simply impossible and thus futile. People cannot be forced to have faith and consequently persecuting them or discriminating against them on the basis of their beliefs in the hope of changing those beliefs is pointless. Religious intolerance is only justified where religious practices threaten state security. In such circumstances, it is not faith that is being regarded intolerantly, but the consequences of actions that spring from faith.

> And if, peradventure, such were the state of affairs, that the interests of the commonwealth required all slaughter of beasts be forborn while, in order to the increasing of the stock of cattle, that had been destroyed by some extraordinary murrain; who sees not that the magistrate in such a case, may forbid all his subjects to kill any calves for any use whatsoever? Only it is to be observed, that in this case the law is made not about a religious but about a political matter: nor is the sacrifice, but the slaughter of calves thereby prohibited.[10]

Locke's clear, simple argument is appealing, and seemingly appropriate to international society by analogy, leaving aside for the time being any concerns about the empirical accuracy of the claim to be unable to coerce faith.[11] Forcibly altering political practices that, for example, breach Western notions of human rights is indefensible, save in the most extreme circumstances when such practices generate general political threats. If we wish to see human rights accepted and respected throughout the world, then this can only be done through winning the argument, rather than by coercively attempting to enforce practices upon states and other political communities that presently reject them. The argument offered by the UK government, for example, that an emphasis on human rights and democracy in foreign policy was doing no more than insisting that others enjoy the same kinds of freedoms that we would insist upon for ourselves fails Locke's test of toleration.[12] A belief in rights and freedoms of a specific sort, as with a belief in a specific instance of religious faith, is not a matter of general concern and to insist that others adopt such beliefs is intolerant and probably ineffectual. If other political communities do not share our 'faith' in human rights and democracy and the consequences of their lack of faith do not generate serious political problems, then they should be left alone.

We might, of course, reject the analogy here by insisting that the idea of human rights stems not from an act of 'faith' but instead from a rigorous, rational intellectual process that meets proper epistemological standards of valid knowledge in a way in which faith cannot. Whilst this is not the place to engage in serious philosophical debate about epistemology and methodology, it is worth noting that the depth of that debate, carried on across the centuries, is a good reason to proceed on the basis that such a resolution is unlikely to gain universal support in the near future. As a result, and even if only for pragmatic reasons, it is necessary to accord epistemological validity to religious and other sorts of belief systems that enjoy significant levels of support. Certainly in the political realm we lack a sustainable and reasonably consensual basis for acting on a different assumption.

Locke's argument requires that the threshold of serious political problems needs to be set high. Human rights abuses, for example, would need to be so serious as to threaten the security of states and perhaps even of international society more generally. This chimes with Hedley Bull's identification of the perpetuation of the society of states as a fundamental goal that may require the forbearance of injustice.[13] Similar arguments exist in political practice. The way in which the UN Security Council has used the idea of 'threats to international peace and security' as a mechanism through which it has attempted to address major humanitarian crises is, in part, a case in point. Whilst the UN Charter means that the Council must use this formulation if it wishes to authorise the use of force, the Council's effort to respond to the crisis in Bosnia, for example, during the mid-1990s would seem to suggest that this is more than a purely pragmatic step.[14] Equally, accommodating the different views of states, like Russia and China, who are extremely cautious regarding the idea of a right to humanitarian intervention, and more enthusiastic advocates, like the United Kingdom, plays its role. The United Kingdom can, for example, offer an interpretation of practice in this area that sees a right to humanitarian intervention emerging and gaining legal standing, as it did in relation to military action over Kosovo and which was also discussed in the case of Iraq in 2003.[15] On the other hand, the Chinese government, and many others, would see military action in places like Bosnia as wholly exceptional, as not setting precedents and certainly not contributing to any sort of general right of humanitarian intervention that states could appeal to in support of unilateral military action.[16]

The idea of addressing only the most serious consequences stemming from ethical diversity and acting in only the most pressing of cases would appear to have utility as an ethic of toleration in a pluralist international society. Academic advocates of a limited right to humanitarian intervention have generally followed this claim, also setting a high hurdle before military action in particular can be justified. However, their reasoning is not always the same as that we are attributing to Locke, who, of course, was principally concerned with toleration within the state. Michael Walzer and Nicholas Wheeler, for example, both set high tests for humanitarian intervention, and both use ideas from the Just War tradition to provide a clear framework of questions to be worked through in making the difficult decisions that always present themselves in these kinds of circumstances.[17]

However, Walzer's test appears, on the face of it, to be different to Locke's. Walzer appeals to the idea of actions which 'shock the moral conscience of mankind', and thus to a seemingly universal test of 'faith' in its belief in some sort of universal standards that would need to exist independently of specific religious faiths or other kinds of belief systems specific to the political communities concerned.[18] Walzer attempts to escape from this problem by arguing for the existence of a meaningful set of universal ethical propositions arising from the overlap between the much richer, or 'thicker' to use Walzer's term, skein of ethical ideas and practices that have grown up within the world's political communities.[19] Walzer is keen to try and avoid 'political community' becoming a synonym for 'state', but, as Chris Brown argues, this is difficult because of the way that Walzer uses a 'legalist paradigm' that refers to states to achieve this goal.[20] This presents problems for thinking about toleration on these grounds when we move beyond the realm of international society and into a world society populated by individuals and non-state-based political actors, networks and groups.[21]

Nevertheless, Walzer appears to offer potential answers to two of the problems that arise from a Lockean approach to toleration. In the case of the first problem – the well-known one of the individual analogy – Walzer offers an account of political community that develops a plausible argument about the ways in which it is possible for us to think about political communities as some sort of corporate moral agent in a way that treats the community's ethics as being more than the sum of the individual parts,[22] and establishes an appeal to the historical social construction of the community and its self-understandings that is compatible with a social constructivist methodology.

The second issue Walzer gains purchase over is that of offering us potentially positive reasons why we should tolerate others. This is a difficulty for a more strictly Lockean position, which can be seen to rely for its defence of the virtue of toleration on the claim that coerced uniformity in crucial matters of faith or other sorts of constitutive beliefs is impossible. Thus, for example, we can argue that Locke tolerates religious diversity because forcibly imposing religious uniformity is impossible. Locke had a definite conception of what he would like to see universalised – a type of Protestantism – and toleration was only a virtue because circumstances conspired to make this impractical. Toleration is prudential or circumstantial, rather than being a positive virtue in its own right.[23] This may also be seen to appeal to a traditional English school pluralism, given the emphasis on prudence as a political virtue to be found there,[24] but given that we have already found this version of pluralism wanting in helping us explore the ethics of territorial borders the move to a more expressly Lockean account of toleration within pluralism seems unlikely to help with this.[25] There seems to be little here that does not once again see territorial borders as simply being the largely uninteresting by-product of sovereignty.

There is one possible exception to this, although this, too, does not help us much in thinking about the ethics of territorial borders, especially in circumstances of globalisation. Were we to base toleration on these kinds of grounds then those forms of political life that threaten the basis of order in international politics are most likely to be found intolerable. The political ramifications of forms of political life that challenge the basis of order and security are unlikely to be forborne, let alone tolerated in the more demanding sense outlined here. For Bull, for example, the principal task of international law was to ensure that there was only one basic set of constitutive principles at work in international politics; in the case of international society, those revolving around sovereign statehood. Forms rejecting this basis are understood as being profoundly dangerous.[26] One manifestation of casting such notions into the category of 'intolerable' is the response to transnational terrorism.

The power of the condemnation of the 9/11 attacks is significantly shaped by a fear of the rejection of the established standards that organisations like Al Qaeda represent. It is not just the scale of the deaths involved. Whilst the death of around 3000 people in a single attack is very large by the standards of terrorist organisations with, for instance, the single worst death toll of the 'Troubles' in Northern Ireland being the 29 people killed at Omagh, in comparison to military operations, 3000 is not an especially high figure. The context of war needs to make an ethical difference in order to help explain the distinction being drawn here and the ethical understanding of war that underpins this difference and also the power of the condemnation of terrorism in Just War thinking.[27]

The development of the Just War tradition has made it inseparable from a sovereign states system because of the way that key notions of right authority, just cause and discrimination have come to be understood. Right authority is linked to the state or, possibly, to an international organisation like the UN that derives its authority in large part from member states.[28] Just cause has been generally restricted to self-defence by states, whether individually or collectively, or revealingly, to the protection of international peace and security which is effectively a synonym for order amongst states. Discrimination in the conduct of military operations rests on the combatant/non-combatant distinction, with combatants being members of the military: that is the armed and uniformed agents of the state.

Whilst Elshtain's defence of US military action after 9/11 is perhaps an extreme example, it is also revealing of the conception of the state that has been placed into the Just War tradition. Elshtain's connection of a liberal, secular, democratic state to the Just War tradition carries with it an argument that just wars are most likely to be fought by states of this type that possess the political institutions, procedures and culture necessary to make the Just War criteria function. By extension, other sorts of political form are a threat to this, not only in their potential unwillingness to abide by, or at least be willing to try and appear to abide by, the rules of the war game, but also because of the potentially radical extension to the use of violence that they might bring. 'Private wars', especially fought using the kinds of techniques associated with terrorism, and carried out by political groups motivated by Manichean and messianic religio-political doctrines, to remind us implicitly that it is certainly not only Islam that has given rise to such views, are profoundly unsettling to international order.[29] The very idea of tolerating such organisations cannot arise on a Lockean basis, because Locke's scheme turns on a liberal distinction between religion and politics, between the faith and the political consequences of that faith. If such a distinction does not exist or cannot be plausibly constructed on even pragmatic grounds, then the scope for toleration becomes desperately narrow.

J. S. Mill seems of more use in constructing a positive liberal argument because he emphasises the virtue of diversity. Mill claims that valuing, even encouraging, diversity in society ensures as many opportunities as possible for progress. The greater the diversity of ideas the greater the chance of only the most fruitful and effective gaining currency in the face of constant challenges from alternatives. Tolerating diversity is not about putting up with that we wish we could change but cannot; instead it is about recognising how diversity prevents society from slipping into conformity, torpor, conservatism and backwardness. Hearing as many voices and seeing as many alternatives as possible protects the creative spark enabling social progress.[30]

This finds something of an echo in Hedley Bull's brand of pluralism, in which he expressed his uncertainty about the claims to superiority of Western, liberal democratic ideas he saw as inherent in a form of cosmopolitanism that he regarded as, essentially, wishful thinking.[31] Instead, Bull urged greater sensitivity towards other cultures although, as we have seen already, this was to be limited by the needs of order and contained within an understanding of international society that is intolerant of political forms that reject the rules of the sovereign state game. Nevertheless, leaving this problem

aside for a moment, Bull argued that the diversity within international society was desirable because it offers different voices against
which we can judge ourselves, and provides different communities
with whom we can interact and from whom we can learn.[32] This
reinforces the prudential concerns about imposing uniformity.

If Bull's enthusiasm for diversity is limited by the need to protect
the constitutive principles and primary institutions of international
society, J. S. Mill's support sometimes appears to approach valuing
eccentricity for eccentricity's sake. However, Mill's teleology of
progress restricts his toleration, in ways that serve to further limit the
idea of toleration that traditional English school pluralists defend,
too. Unlike Locke, Mill only offers a weak reason why we should
tolerate that of which we morally disapprove. Locke's answer is the
impossibility of coercing genuine belief (although he does not
extend such licence to action resulting from such beliefs). Mill's
answer is weak because of the way in which he stresses the purpose
of toleration as being to foster progress and improvement in society.
A strong prescriptive element informs Mill's conception of progress –
predicated upon the principles of utilitarian liberalism – meaning
that the licence of toleration within society is ultimately rather
limited.

The scope of toleration is likely to narrow over time as progress
occurs. The need for diversity in order to provide us with different
ideas from which we can learn, different social and political models
against which we can judge ourselves and with which we can
interact ought to become less as time goes on. A kind of iterative
process occurs in which basic social and political principles become
refined and established and leeway remains only over the best ways
of implementing such principles, and here diversity may well be
desirable and appropriate in recognition of different local circumstances. This may give rise to things which we do not like about
how our political community or other political communities are
run. We may have preferences for proportional electoral systems,
bicameral parliaments, written constitutions, extensive public
ownership of basic utilities and health care facilities and so on
across a whole host of other political matters. However, this is to
forbear that which we do not like about other iterations of the basic
liberal model; only rarely do such questions turn on matters that
may raise more fundamental ethical questions. There are examples

in areas such as abortion, the death penalty, medical research and military technology, but even here the emphasis within liberal political systems on procedural as well as substantive matters of justice provides a mechanism for containing the consequences of these disputes. Thus we can ethically condemn the death penalty, research into biological weaponry and bans on therapeutic cloning and abortion (for the sake of argument) but accept that different polities can reach different conclusions about these and that the political processes through which those decisions gain public force are acceptable ones and that there are mechanisms by which they can be changed. We may not like it, we may take steps to bring pressure to bear to change it, we may question the moral integrity of those holding such beliefs, but, for the most part, we accept the outcome because it is the result of proper procedure. Those who do not, such as violent anti-vivisection organisations, find themselves facing the coercive force of the state.

Therefore the inherent vision of the good life – the answer to the classic political theoretical question of 'How should we live?' – within Mill's liberalism restricts what at first sight appears to be a positive defence of toleration. The individualism, the belief in the public/private divide, the particular vision of political participation and the utilitarianism of Mill's political philosophy make it inimical to those who do not share this vision of the good life. Whether in pluralist or cosmopolitan guise, the arguments for the purely derivative ethical significance of territorial borders make the same sort of claim. For pluralists, diversity is tolerable within states, up to the point where it potentially threatens the basis of order in international society, including when that diversity escapes from the container of the territorially bordered state to produce aspects of world society that challenge order, too. For cosmopolitans, the distinction between international and world society is less important, indeed for some it may even be ethically irrelevant, but the containment of diversity and the limitation of it to variations on the cosmopolitan theme takes place just the same. Territorial borders may be less prominent and their ethical contingency more clearly stated, but they endure by marking off areas of political authority and carry ethical weight in the way in which cosmopolitan schemes discriminate between different claims to political authority on the basis of accordance with cosmopolitan values.

David Blaney and Naeem Inayatullah have talked helpfully of 'the Westphalian deferral' of the diversity issue in international politics.[33] This highlights the way in which the issue of ethical diversity was not answered at Westphalia, even in the mythologised version of the treaty common in international relations, but instead deferred by being shunted into the 'domestic' or 'unit' level. International society would be homogenous – based on the idealised notion of the sovereign state, or, under the impact of nationalism, the idealised sovereign nation-state – with diversity corralled within the state, where it would be covered by the norms of non-intervention, territorial integrity and other deeply rooted elements of what has become the international legal system. The pressure for cosmopolitan approaches to international relations, perhaps especially those drawing on a broadly liberal tradition, have, as we have seen, rendered this deferral unstable, reinforced by the development of a global economy, technological transformations and the rest of the globalisation agenda that is altering the material and, more importantly, the ideational basis upon which conceptions of international and global politics rest.

If the collapsing deferral of the diversity question is another challenge adding to the idea of a 'Westfailure' system, then the pressure to complete the abandonment of the idea of territorial borders as possessing ethical significance would appear to be further reinforced.[34] A positive ethical defence must explain how territorial borders can give us reason to tolerate not just that which we might not like, but that which we ethically reject, without resulting in a relativism that requires us to tolerate everything. There must be a mechanism for identifying the intolerable, too. On the basis of this short survey, liberalism does not look like a promising line of enquiry, reiterating prudential and pragmatic arguments via Locke, and contingent ones via Mill. Within these approaches radical alternative challenges may be forborne, but they are not tolerated in the richer sense of being valued, of having their views protected and engaged with, even if that engagement may ultimately result in rejection.

A richer concept of toleration

If we are to escape from contingency and a swallowing up of territorial borders in concepts such as sovereignty, instead following the arguments from political geography about the inherent importance of territorial borders, then we need a richer ethical exploration. This must be more open to alternative conceptions of the good life, of the ontological status of human beings and able to accommodate a wider array of actors without losing an ability to recognise the different levels of sedimentation they enjoy in the political system. As part of this it must be able to recognise the power of bordering behaviour that the political geography and anthropology work considered earlier highlights, recognising that whilst this takes many forms other than the territorial, territorial borders are one important manifestation of this powerful political act. Finally, it must also protect what is essential by identifying what is intolerable.

This is a very tall order indeed, and whilst this book hopes to make significant progress in generating one sort of answer to this question it would be presumptuous to assume that this is the only or necessarily the best answer. Questions such as this are never likely to generate long-standing consensus, although it is perhaps testament to the power of the Westphalian answer that it has become so entrenched in most ways of thinking about this problem. However, the reasons to be dissatisfied with the Westphalian solution, or deferral, appear compelling and the way out via an argument for ethical contingency problematic in a number of important ways, including a failure to seriously question the portrayal of territorial borders in ways that are similar to the 'territorial trap' from which they offer a supposed escape.

What is needed is a way to recognise the value that exists in the social practices of territorial bordering and not to assume this is subsumed within sovereignty. Seeing territorial borders as partially constitutive of a toleration of difference and diversity in human societies that addresses the weaknesses of a liberal notion offers a way of dealing with radical difference, even in the forms of hatred, prejudice and conflict. We may wish to live in a world in which hatred, prejudice and conflict have been banished, but that cannot be a reason to ignore or dismiss what are, undeniably, among the most powerful motivations for political action and which remain prominent in political conduct. Genuine toleration – living and engaging with that we find ethically troubling – requires a better way of understanding and addressing these 'negative' forces in political life. International and global politics ask the questions in their most difficult forms, too, because it is at the global level that diversity is at its greatest and where the scope for the political workings out of that diversity are increasingly taking place: both tolerant and intolerant, and intolerable. The race for the state and the bastions of Just War may be one response to transnational terrorism, but it can offer little in the way of long-term mechanisms for addressing the violent threats and challenges of a globalising world, even for the most powerful state on the planet, and let alone for the rest of us.[35]

The starting point for this part of the argument lies in the political theory of Hannah Arendt. This is not an obvious place to begin, perhaps, as Arendt wrote very little about international politics, certainly if we restrict ourselves to systematic efforts to engage with the field. Much of what Arendt did say about international relations was, unsurprisingly, placed firmly in the context of the Cold War, which only entered its first, partial, thaw during the period of détente as Arendt was approaching the end of her life (she died in 1975). As a result, on the face of it the few observations she offers would fit into a straightforward realist account, emphasising the role of military force as underpinning international politics and seeing it as an arena so overshadowed by the possibility of massive, exterminating violence via nuclear war as to be largely beyond hope as a site for politics as she understood it.[36]

The potential benefits of turning to Arendt are significant though, both in this context and more generally. Certainly, recent work by Douglas Klusmeyer has highlighted the way in which Arendt offers ways of thinking about questions of power and the nature of political action that mark her out from the realism of her contemporaries, in particular, Hans Morgnethau and George Kennan. Arendt's analysis of the Holocaust plays a vital role in the ways in which Klusmeyer argues in favour of seeing Arendt as a 'critical realist', able to offer insights that eluded Morgenthau and Kennan who, he argues, failed to fully appreciate the political significance of totalitarianism in general and the Holocaust in particular.[37] This also gives Arendt a particular grip on the idea of evil in politics, something that has been prominent in discussions of post-9/11 transnational politics. However, rather than evil being in some sense apolitical – a radically different or 'other' political force that is beyond comprehension – we can instead begin to see it as politically significant and serious, something that we must think about with care.[38]

Arendt's account of totalitarianism links with her more general account of what she labels 'plurality' – the diversity of individuals – and 'pluralism' – the diversity of communities. In particular, plurality is regarded by Arendt as the basic ontological fact of human existence. '[W]e are all the same, that is, human, in such a way that nobody is ever the same as anyone else who ever lived, lives or will live.'[39] This, in one sense, makes Arendt a cosmopolitan, because she offers a universal proposition about human beings, and one with great ethical import, too. However, because this proposition is about the essential difference between each and every one of us, Arendt is able to offer us a way of thinking in universal or cosmopolitan terms that does not require us to make assumptions about the outcome of such thinking being universal rights. Instead, the possibility of this plurality manifesting itself in ways that generate quite sharply different workings through of the issue of the moral standing of individuals and, as we shall see, communities becomes possible. This is, however, limited by the need to acknowledge the way in which plurality is connected to community and by the basic claim that plurality cannot sustain a denial of human status to others.

Plurality requires the existence of multiple perspectives if it is to have meaning in the real lives of real people. We cannot understand who we are, in contrast to what we are, outside of the condition of pluralism – outside of the condition of membership of a political community. To acquire meaning we need to encounter different ways of looking at things that come through interaction with other humans with whom we share some things in common and with whom we interact through speech. 'The impossibility . . . to solidify in words the living essence of the person as it shows itself in the flux of action and speech, has great bearing on the whole realm of human affairs, where we exist primarily as acting and speaking beings.'[40] However, we all bring something different to bear, some distinctive take on the world that we inhabit and share with other human beings and with whom we build communities and shared identities. This is not the pluralism of the English school, as it is usually understood, or of an ethno-nationalist arguing for separateness through historical experience and shared 'blood'.[41] Those approaches portray the diversity of human beings and of their communities as the result of history, whether accidental or not, or as a by-product of the anarchic states-system. Instead, here we can begin to see diversity as something that cannot be deferred or shut away within the territorial confines of the state. Here it is something that has to be addressed head on.

Plurality's central position in the human condition and the nature of political action does not, though, preclude comprehensibility and understanding amongst individuals, otherwise they could not form communities, or between diverse communities, otherwise a key source of the dynamic of politics would be lost.[42] Neither is this comprehensibility limited in some way to a political elite, trained in the art of diplomacy and steeped in diplomatic culture. Arendt's take on politics is to see it as the highest form of human activity, the arena in which individuals can seize the opportunity to reveal who they really are by acting on the public stage and potentially setting in train processes that bring about change. The opportunity to engage with others, in a trusting and trustworthy fashion, requires a set of shared ideas and understandings that are the product of interaction and are at their strongest within well-established communities.[43] Plurality is not just individualism, therefore, and Arendt sees humans as rooted, conditioned creatures, the product of a process that takes place within communities that are vital, in the sense of being both alive and dynamic, as well as being crucial to the creation of each, diverse, person.[44]

This kind of socialisation does not overwrite or homogenise the plurality of people, though, as difference and diversity within communities is at least as great as that between communities. But in order to recognise difference, and to act politically requires such a recognition, we must know who we are by comparison and engagement with others with whom we share much in common.[45]

Arendt is no nationalist, though. Whilst undoubtedly primarily a theorist of the bounded community, perhaps helping explain her relative neglect in international relations, her account of history stresses that the idea of separate, national histories characterised by a communal teleology leading in the direction of some sort of national destiny is a modern aberration.[46] It is, though, a powerful aberration, offering grounding for idealised, fixed and permanent territorial boundaries and this has to be included in our account of politics. The construction of territorial borders is therefore a part of the plurality of human beings that cannot be transcended, yet they are only one element of constructed, flexible and dynamic notions of identity and belonging. These are unpredictable, too, given the nature of political action as Arendt describes it, with her idea of 'natality' appealing to the unpredictable and limitless potential nascent in every human birth.[47]

Escaping from the construction of pluralism via nationalism or some other homogenised communal identity, such as Huntington's notion of 'civilization', and from the idea of an essential universalism that sustains universal political meanings and forms, such as rights, Arendt marks out a highly distinctive position.[48] It is especially useful in this context because of the way that we are asked to look at plurality as inescapable and essential to meaningfulness in human affairs. As a result, valuing and protecting plurality becomes an ethical imperative for our political systems. Human politics, at least as it ought to be experienced, cannot be reduced to sterile notions of 'clashes' between essentialised and reified units, whether they be nations, states or civilisations. The diversity of the human condition goes far wider than these efforts to accommodate or explain it allow, because it is at the heart of the human condition. The plurality of people, the pluralism of their communities, which are not just states, and the institutions where this is worked out, including international and transnational locations, are all connected by this appeal to diversity.

Thus understanding political action and the ways in which we can respond to other political movements, actors and ideas cannot take place on the basis of abstract universals. Arendt offers an excellent example of this, in the ways in which she reflected on the Holocaust.[49] She appealed to her self-recognition as a Jew, an identity inextricable from social and political circumstances contributing to the idea, and a contested idea, of Jewishness, as a basis upon which Nazism could be resisted. This was contrasted with those critical of specific identity as a source of resistance, preferring instead to appeal to 'humanity'. 'Those who reject such identifications', Arendt wrote, 'may feel wonderfully superior to the world..., but their superiority is...the superiority of a more or less well-equipped cloud cuckoo land.'[50]

Thus even, indeed especially, a political movement like Nazism cannot be treated as somehow *sui generis*, a political form or movement that is in some way 'evil' and thus beyond consideration as a part of the human world. Neither, though, can it be comprehended simply as a more extreme version of power-maximising politics.[51]

Equally, an appeal to an abstract, idealised, de-politicised ethical notion like humanity or human rights offers little hope as a basis for effective resistance. Arendt's 'Origins of Totalitarianism' offers one of the most powerful critiques of the human rights ideal, drawing in part on her own experience as a stateless refugee to appeal to one, single universal right – the right to have rights.[52]

By this she means the right to belong to a political community which can grant meaning, specificity and effectiveness to the idea of being a rights holder. Totalitarian projects that would deny the right of a whole people to exist are so terrifying because they deny them their plurality as individuals. She describes the genocide against the Jews as '... an attack upon human diversity as such, that is, upon a characteristic of the "human status" without which the very words "mankind" or "humanity" would be devoid of meaning'.[53] It is for this reason, she argues in her famous and controversial account of his trial, that Adolf Eichmann deserved to die. The 'banality of evil' – that famous phrase with which she tried to sum up the lessons of the Eichmann trial, and which caused her so much trouble in the Jewish community, reduced genocide to bureaucracy, with its attendant trivia, turf fights and disputes. Fighting against this through the appeal to community, to diversity, offers a far more effective tool than the abstract appeal to humanity that, although to very different effect and with very different meaning, produces a downplaying of human diversity, too, and thus of humanity.

Concluding her analysis of totalitarianism, Arendt emphasises its destruction not just of public life, as tyrannies had done before, but of private life as well. 'Loneliness' – the utter isolation of individuals from their communities under totalitarianism – destroys the human ability to participate in meaningful relationships with one another. 'What makes loneliness so unbearable is the loss of one's own self which can be realized in solitude, but confirmed in its identity only by the trusting and trustworthy company of my equals. In this situation, man loses trust in himself as the partner of his thoughts and that elementary confidence in the world which is necessary to make experiences at all.'[54] Without community and involvement, human identity and the potential for action, Arendt's definition of freedom, is unprotected.[55]

Formulaic and bureaucratic mechanisms to protect freedom are therefore largely unattractive to Arendt. Political institutions have to come from an act of popular will, they have to be the result of action, as she portrays it. The pre-eminent form of such action is the founding of a republic, the making of a new political place by individuals who have come to share the basis of trust through promising and forgiving that will enable them to create and, hopefully, sustain the ideals that lead them to want to create a common political home. Her analysis of the French and American revolutions emphasises how the French revolution lost the ability to sustain its ideals, at least in comparison with the US revolution, in important part because of the abandonment of the local, the active and the rooted in favour of the grand principle and the central direction.[56] The French Revolution's Declaration of the Rights of Men and of Citizens is also a key text in her analysis of the development of human rights, crucial for the way in which, Arendt argues, it highlights the contradiction between the ideas of possessing rights through being human and possessing rights through being a citizen, with the latter being the only meaningful sense.[57]

The disengagement of individuals from the political process is an aspect of modern politics that Arendt highlights. Indeed, she goes so far as to argue that most Western thinking about politics is not really about politics at all. Instead it is about 'ruling' – the process whereby political decision-making moves away from the people and becomes an increasingly specialised, bureaucratised and isolated activity, carried out by a small political elite appealing to certain sorts of idealised political blueprints. These serve to remove the need for political involvement from the great mass of people and turns politics into 'work', requiring 'political craftsmen', rather than an opportunity for political action.[58] Instead, the successful polity needs to retain its attachment to the communities, identities and founding ideals that gave it direction and impetus in the first place. These cannot be pickled in aspic, unchanging for ever more, because that is not the nature of political action.[59] The potential for action to have unpredictable and far-reaching consequences is always present, and is what helps to make promising – setting up islands of certainty in the ocean of uncertainty that is the future – and forgiving – allowing ourselves and others to move on from past wrongs – cardinal political virtues.[60]

This idea of a genuine, 'worldly' politics distinguishes Arendt from the liberal political agenda and gives her an unusual take on the idea of toleration, too.[61] The dismissal of abstract, philosophical bases for virtues such as toleration appeals to their lack of grounding in a reality that is the result of human activity and history that is socially constructed. Appeals to universality are possible, but only through sharing values via discourse and interaction, rather than through the assertion of abstract principles. To be effective, political principles must come from human action and not from thought alone.

Arendt's ideal political system is the Athenian agora, although she realises that the practical possibility of recreating such a system is long since passed. Nevertheless, appealing to the agora's politics of participation runs strongly through her thought, a wish that we could aspire to this spirit of action. Conceptual rigidity and over-concentration on institutions damage what she labels the 'space in-between', the ephemeral, transitory and inter-subjective place where individuals can come together in order to make things happen, to act politically and to confirm themselves in their identity and in their sharing of a community. '[T]he world and the people who inhabit it are not the same. The world lies between people, and this in-between . . . is today the object of the greatest concern and the most obvious upheaval in all the countries of the globe.'[62] Engaging openly and fully with the different, with diversity, is the way we engage with ourselves. We need to act in the world, to open ourselves to engagement with those with whom we are familiar and with those with whom we are not.

This move enables us to utilise in a novel way the methodological space that constructivism opens. Rather than seeking to reconceptualise borders as ethically contingent social constructs within a broader ethic of either order in anarchy and a statist notion of diversity on the one hand, or as downgraded and increasingly by-passed hangovers in a globalising world on the other, we can locate them within an essential plurality. In particular, tying this to the critique of essentialised, Westphalian territorial borders in political geography enables us to consider territorial borders as possessing ethical significance in and of themselves as a necessary part of the working out of an Arendtian idea of plurality, tied to a virtue of toleration that is much more than the limited, liberal versions we have looked at and which are manifested in the pluralist and solidarist ethical critiques of territorial borders we considered earlier.

As Arendt notes, it is discourse and interaction, not humanity, that links people together: 'For the world is not humane just because it is made by human beings, and it does not become humane just because the human voice sounds within it, but only when it has become the object of discourse.'[63] The space in-between individuals, communities and institutions, increasingly not just within the state but across states, in the space of world society, is where discourse can take place, where identities can meet, generating a more genuine humanity. As well as challenging efforts, for example by Jackson, to channel the interaction of diversity through the institutions of international society, limiting participation to a tiny number of 'elite' individuals, Arendt's approach opens space for other voices, too.[64] The idea of an 'in-between' liberated from the institutional and spatial confines of the state through the idea of globalisation and the opening of the space of world society gives a greater opportunity for the victims of power to be heard, extending the ability of our thinking to recognise pluralism and plurality in world politics and encouraging us to engage with a far richer spectrum of diversity than that privileged by a traditional pluralism that is focused too tightly on the state.[65]

Thinking along these lines enables us to return territorial borders to the world. Sedimented and reified features like territorial borders can instead be re-politicised by thinking of them in relation to the creation of the space in-between where political action can occur and real politics takes place. We can get away from the 'border-as-fence' analogy and view them as devices for creating a space in-between, rather than a perimeter maintained and policed by a small diplomatic, political and military elite. This has served to close off politics into separate realms and forms, with politics occurring in one mode within states and in a different one between them. Returning these realms to a human politics of diversity requires constant questioning of their legitimacy and role, including of the devices that separate them. This occurs via active political involvement through the discourse of real individuals and real communities, not by judgement against either abstract absolute standards or an elitist monolith of diplomatic custom and practice.

Arendt berates the shutting off of political space in modern politics, contributing to the 'unworldliness' of liberalism that also infects liberalism's approach to toleration.[66] The space in-between does not possess the teleology or moral ontology of individuality that characterises Mill's approach, for example. Instead, we need to recognise and engage the political aspects of a much greater range of human activity, including that we abhor. Toleration in this vein is much greater than that coming out of liberalism. Hatred, prejudice and conflict, for example, matter to individuals and their communities. These are significant forces and ones that a worldly politics has to take seriously, rather than simply condemning. A genuine discourse involves hearing and considering these views, not declaring ourselves abstract, individual members of a great human collectivity to whom such things are a 'false consciousness', or irrational or abhorrent and thus unworthy of serious consideration.

Recognising these negative forces in politics gives us a reason to tolerate them – they are as important to the human experience as commitments to equality, liberty and justice – and this makes recognition and engagement unavoidable. Understanding, interaction, dialogue and a recognition of human weakness, as well as heroism, are essential to a worldliness recognising the space in-between human beings, their communities and institutions as *the* site of politics. Territorial borders potentially play a role in establishing these in-betweens, not because they divide sovereignties, with the state being the place where equality, liberty and justice can flourish, but because they are a part of the pluralism of human communities. There is a need for division and distinction between communities, and this can take, and frequently has taken, a territorial form. This territorial form does not have to be via exclusive sovereignty, but this has proven to be a durable and attractive mechanism, and, despite the undoubted costs that cosmopolitan critics are quick to highlight, such durability and attractiveness ought not to be dismissed out of hand.

Additionally, territorial borders play a role in limiting politics, too, and this is an important part of any political theory and a vital question of political ethics. Given Arendt's central concern with totalitarianism it is no surprise that she was deeply concerned with limits in politics, stemming in part from her claim that civilisation is neither inevitable, or even terribly secure in the face of human hubris and the tendency of human introduced trends to run out of control.[67] Territorial borders as elements of community and as ways of dividing and dissipating institutional power, whilst accepting the difficulty of maintaining clear, definitional lines in an unpredictable and dynamic human political environment, respond to the challenge of political geography. It also, though, responds to the challenge of international political theory's concern with the ethical and the normative. We can retain a recognition of the pluralist argument that territorial borders divide political and military might, helping resist totalising imperial projects that threaten the order of international society, but go further than this, too. In particular, Arendt saw territorial borders as helping to establish limits that can rob totalitarianism of its dynamism and undermine its political tactic of 'permanent revolution' through which it is able to galvanise support, sweeping away prior political forms, engendering the 'loneliness' that, before physical extermination, robs individuals of the political location that makes them properly human.[68]

However, territorial borders must be a part of the unpredictable, evolutionary political dynamic that can only come about through real communities, changing to reflect the developments of these communities. To the extent that territorial borders have provided an institutional focus for the accretion of rules on violence in international politics they ought also to receive ethical endorsement. The wielding of violent military might is the single greatest threat to Arendt's conception of politics, hence, perhaps, her disregard of an international relations that, in her lifetime, had been dominated by the military might of the Third Reich and of the nuclear stand-off of the Cold War. Violence, Arendt argued, is politically null, even anti-political, crushing the properly political space of the in-between and rendering meaningless the virtues of promising and forgiveness.[69] Territorial borders can therefore help to hold open discursive space by providing a location around which controls can grow, giving them a spatial focus and location that also appeals to the historically well-entrenched practice of communities identifying themselves in territorial ways to at least some extent.

It may possibly be the case that the development of globalisation will eventually result in a transformation so extensive that this historical pattern of territorialising community is broken. However, the prospect of a wholly supraterritorial global society seems remote and the role of territorial borders as constitutive of important human communities rooted in the plurality of individuals, their social need for belonging and their political need for recognition and status looks likely to continue. This does not preclude 'post-Westphalian', or neo-medieval political orders, or require a hard-line attachment to the notion of sovereignty that resulted from de-colonisation. Partially detaching territorial borders from sovereignty recreates the possibility of thinking about them as important social institutions in their own right and thus enabling an exploration of the ethics that are entangled in the choices that we can make about the role and status of territorial borders, and not just the question of where they should be drawn or what security functions they should fulfil.[70]

In terms of this argument about their possessing an ethic of toleration that responds to deep-rooted difference and diversity in human society, territorial borders can give us reasons to tolerate that we reject, not just on prudential grounds, but for more substantive reasons. Toleration as part of a worldly, political process of engagement with and recognition for others is about more than forbearance. The risks are familiar – granting a platform to extremists, racists, bigots and the whole panoply of derogatory terms applied to views we find offensive. This price needs to be paid, though, not because we cannot change such views, as Locke might argue, but because these views are a part of the human political experience. Arendt, for example, was criticised for her opposition to forced de-segregation of schools in the US south, arguing that the only role that the state should play was to protect constitutionally enshrined rights, which the Supreme Court achieved through its ruling that declared segregation illegal. Beyond this, imposing social uniformity through bussing and other actions was intolerant.[71]

Toleration, of course, cannot be limitless. It only makes sense to talk of toleration if there are things that are intolerable. The violent refusal to reciprocate toleration is intolerable because the resort to violence marks an end to the political process. This flies in the face of one of the most famous dicta in international politics – Clausewitz's claim that war is the continuation of politics by other means – but that is a view of politics that emphasises power and its exercise over others, which, as we have seen, is more in tune with 'ruling' in Arendt's terms.[72] It also, of course, raises all kinds of ethical difficulties in relation to the 'legitimate' or 'just' or 'ethical' resort to war that the Just War tradition attempts to address. In particular, both Clausewitz and Just War thinking, along with international law, privilege the violence carried out by the state. It is states that are the 'legitimate authority' of the *jus ad bellum*, for instance; war is distinguished from private violence or, to borrow a typically pithy phrase, the 'recreational brigandage' that Colin Gray sees in the violence associated with paramilitary groups in conflicts such as Bosnia, Sierra Leone or Liberia.[73] Certainly one of the points of the label 'terrorism' is to de-legitimise the perpetrators by distinguishing them from the legitimate violence of the state. Efforts by Irish Republicans to place the British army in the same category as the Irish Republican Army (IRA) in discussions of the de-militarisation of Northern Irish politics is one example of the effort to challenge this privileging. Equally, the Unionist insistence of speaking of 'Sinn Fein IRA' is the mirror image effort to delegitimise a political party through its association with a paramilitary 'private' army.

However, we must recognise that intolerant violence is frequently the preserve of the state and that an appeal to the role of territorial borders as devices for toleration has to be aware that debates about war, violence, terrorism and so on must include the state, too. Indeed, a refusal to reciprocate toleration and a policy of armed, violent repression is often at its most extreme when carried out by the state because of the resources it can mobilise. The challenge in international relations, though, is how to respond to violent repression. Pacifism is not a stance that appealed to Arendt, and her realism meant that her political theory grew out of, rather than stood separate from, the conduct of politics in the world around her. It could, perhaps, hardly be otherwise given her personal experience. Thus there are times when the resort to violence becomes unavoidable, especially in the face of those who have themselves abandoned toleration are an intent on the violent imposition of force. As Hansen notes in his discussion of Arendt's political thought, her position meant that 'Political equality requires a minimum threshold: that all must have access to the public world.'[74] Violently enforcing political homogeneity is therefore intolerable, with Arendt even defending the right of Adolf Eichmann to be heard at his trial, taking seriously his arguments and finally defending the death penalty because of Eichmann's denial of the Jews' right to exist, to participate in a political process.[75]

This kind of richer version of toleration, an emphasis on access to the political world, an Arendtian sensibility about the nature of politics, a resistance to repressive violence and an active valuing of diversity can generate important political consequences. These are as good reasons as, for example, human rights, for intervening in the face of human suffering, for example, because they encompass and value the discourse of human rights without restricting an ethical stance to a human rights one. Such a justification for action may be more politically acceptable, too, because it does not privilege an abstract and monolithic notion of human moral agency, instead allowing, indeed positively requiring, a debate and discussion about this amongst those willing and able to take a political stance. This deepens liberal concerns with the non-reciprocity of toleration, taking what is in some ways a distinctly liberal argument and situating it in a discourse that is essential to meaning and a sense of reality in human affairs.

We can therefore use this to think about the idea of territorial borders in the context of humanitarian intervention. In particular, the idea of humanitarianism is one that is often taken to be almost apolitical, associated with a commitment to charity, to neutrality and impartiality, exemplified in the work of the International Committee of the Red Cross (ICRC).[76] On the account offered here, being human, and therefore the potential for humanitarianism, becomes about creating access to political space. This, of course, presupposes the existence of minima of security, but the relieving of distress and the provision of succour are not the end of the matter. In order to enable people to regain their humanity they must have access to political space and that come only through the lifting of the terror of loneliness and the creation of a community. Part of the creation of community is likely to be the creation, or securing, or restoring of territorial borders around that community, of a sense of location and place that are part of the grounding of ethical traditions. As Arendt herself once noted, 'Human dignity needs a new guarantee which can only be found in a new political principle, in a new law on earth, whose validity ... must comprehend the whole of humanity whilst its power must remain strictly limited, rooted in and controlled by newly defined territorial entities.'[77]

The universal requirement for respect for community – 'the right to have rights' – the need for mechanisms that enable diversity to be tolerated, rather than merely forborne, enable the drawing of lines to be understood as an ethically significant practice, as a part of the process of creating political space, and as a social institution that can exist separate from sovereignty or other dominant frameworks within which territorial borders have been placed. Where territorial borders, and the rules and norms attached to them, are being used in defence of violent intolerance, or as a mechanism to shield violent intolerance from others on the grounds that they are 'foreigners', then they can and even should be breached. Intervention can be a humanitarian act, not just because it may serve to bring an end to appalling human suffering and misery, but because it may also recreate the basis for a human politics, a politics that includes pluralism of communities and the desirability of difference.

There are no guarantees of this outcome, of course. The absence or corruption of good intentions, the immense complexity of intervening in extremely difficult circumstances, hubris and mistake may all serve to render an intervention either a failure or alternatively serve to prevent states from acting when they should have done. Somalia and Rwanda may serve as examples of these two outcomes respectively from the perspective of humanitarian intervention.[78]

Whilst this access to the political world has been discussed so far in the context of the state, and, of course, Arendt was a theorist of the bounded community, little interested in international relations, the pressure of globalisation means that access cannot just be about the state. The connections between a world society populated by individuals, international non-governmental organisations, transnational corporations and a plethora of other actors and less tangible networks make unsustainable the argument that it is through the state, and only the state, that we can engage politically. Equally, hopes, either on the part of citizens or on the part of political leaders, that the state can protect us from the consequences of the workings out of global diversity and insulate us especially from the violent aspects of this seem utopian.[79]

'Giving in' to terror is not just about political leaderships conceding to terrorist demands. The argument here suggests that we can also 'give in' by living in fear, especially if that fear become a generalised fear of a specific community. For example , in the aftermath of the bomb attacks in London in July 2005, a great deal of effort was made by political and religious leaders to disassociate Islam from suicide bombing and to argue that resisting such association was an important part of defeating the political objectives of terrorist organisations.[80] We do not have to accept the validity of violently intolerant individuals who take upon themselves, even in the name of religious authority, the duty to kill others, and often themselves, too, in the age of the suicide bomber. More important is the need to place this in the context of the need for channels of communication and engagement.

Elshtain is right to argue that those who seek to take onto the United States, or 'the West' more generally, blame for the September 11 attacks are misguided.[81] Those who hijacked the planes and planned the operation cannot be absolved of responsibility, they were not helpless automata in some sort of structurally determined conflict. A dismissal as 'evil' or 'totalitarian' or 'fanatical' or some other epithet will not do, either. If we are to understand what happened, we must engage with it, and that means facing up the extent of diversity, the real pluralism of political community, and the fallibility and unpredictability of the political institutions through which we mediate human plurality.

These institutions include those of international society, and include territorial borders. They also include the institutions of a world society that, as Barry Buzan points out, many advocates wish to see as almost wholly benign in order to strengthen a normative case that ought really to be tempered with a recognition of the downside of such global phenomena.[82] This is most easily done in the case of transnational terrorist and criminal groups, with the sometimes hazy distinction between the two, given the need to finance terrorist activity and the criminal nature of some of that financing. However, violent reactions are generated by all sorts of social activity in the new social and political spaces of globality, even to the very idea of globalisation itself in the shape of the protests that accompany G-8, World Bank and IMF gatherings.

The record of appeals to transcending, universal ideals such as 'humanitarianism' in order to overcome resistance, break down barriers and establish commonality is not particularly impressive. Certainly, those efforts to use such ideals in the most difficult of political circumstances show they are not immune from inclusion in a political world, and in a violent, intolerant and oppressive political world, too. The claim to be acting for humanitarian reasons or in pursuit of humanitarian goals has not protected Western workers from kidnap and execution in Iraq and did not protect United Nations Protection Force (UNPROFOR) and other UN missions in the

1990s from manipulation, extortion, subversion and aggression on the part of those rejecting their authority, suspicious of their actions or simply extremely determined to pursue their objectives irrespective of any condemnation heaped upon them. There may be those who regard resistance to the forces of global liberal democratic capitalism as being futile, with assimilation to some extent or other being inevitable, but there appear to be a great many people in the world who are not yet convinced of this, and finding better ways of engaging with these views is very important. The stress on inclusion that comes from the liberal tradition or from the idea of ideal communication associated with the Habermasian take on critical theory or Richard Shapcott's advocacy of Gadamer's version of hermeneutics appears the obvious, perhaps only, way forward.[83]

However, exclusion should not be rejected out of hand as unavoidably negative in the face of this challenge of diversity. A Westphalian, pluralist *modus vivendi* is crumbling, losing its credibility in the face of globalisation, humanitarian emergencies and the emergence of transnational terrorism. However, this is not the only way we can exclude on a territorial basis and the depth, strength and durability of territorial borders as social practices should give us pause for thought before consigning them to the dustbin of history. An ethical exploration of territorial borders as imbued with an ethic of toleration restores proper significance to territorial borders, recognising the multiplicity of roles and functions that they play and their significance to the human condition and the centrality of plurality to this condition. More practically, we can recognise the role that territorial borders play in efforts to create a tolerant, worldly politics of diversity where the politically mute, but nevertheless less loud, voice of violence is heard less often.

Conclusion

This account of the status of territorial borders and of their potential to act as part of a system of toleration, although of a rather different kind than that normally associated with a liberal notion of toleration, has highlighted the depth and complexity of the issues involved. It has not, indeed probably could not, offered some sort of definitive statement of *the* way in which this has to be worked out. Nevertheless, following through the idea of territorial borders as social practices producing constitutive rules of international politics, connecting this to critiques of the Westphalian form of that social practice, recognising the power of the critical geographical claims for reconsideration of borders and drawing on the normative and ethical turn in international relations has led us in, hopefully, interesting directions.

Certainly some important ethical questions have been posed, such as the value and desirability of territorial borders as devices of exclusion, the place of diversity in political life, ways in which we can think about the toleration that diversity necessitates, and how we can nevertheless establish limits to politics, in this case through the idea of the intolerable. The emphasis here has been on an approach that borrows from and is indebted to Hannah Arendt's political theory, although her relative lack of interest in international relations has meant that a deal of licence in the interpretation and use of her ideas has to be sought. It is also necessary to recognise the differences between the political circumstances with which she was primarily concerned and the international political realm. This is both an empirical judgement about the enduring influence of anarchy in generating politics of a different character to that within the well-ordered state, and also, and more importantly, a recognition of the power of the idea of such a difference. Division and bordering are particularly important here and have taken on especial significance through the globalisation of the states-system. The actorly qualities of the players on the international and global stages are also different from those within the state. States are not individuals and the individual analogy brings with it substantial costs in terms of analytical penetration. Similarly, the actors populating world society are not accurately reduced to analogues of individual human beings. Arendt's stress on the rootedness and location of individuals, distinguished from the atomised individualism of liberalism, has proven helpful here, by enabling thinking about ways in which the nature and status of individuality are mediated through membership of political communities as an essential mechanism not just for identity or belonging, but for meaning to find a place in human life.

If the analytical and ideational anchors of the Westphalian system are coming adrift then we have not only an opportunity to add to our conceptual repertoire in seeking to understand change and explore the new conditions of globality, world society and the like, but also to reconsider older ideas and how they are amenable to change and the consequences for the role they play. As so many, if not all, of the constitutive rules and institutions of international politics are primarily ideational then this change is not immune from human agency, it is not the product of materially determined forces and structures. Thus the question of ethics arises and the need for a normative compass that can at least identify the different directions available, even if it is unable to pick out the true direction of travel in the face of innumerable possibilities and deep division over the location of the destination.

The need for meaning in life through membership of a community and the opportunities that this offers for properly political action gives us grounds to take the ethical significance of territorial borders seriously, and not to see them as possessing merely contingent significance. The need to place limits has such deep connections with territory, with the idea of borders between those within and those without that carry some sort of special significance, even if it is not sovereignty, that an explanation that explores beyond the instrumental, beyond the bureaucratic capability of political authority, for instance, is essential. The role of territorial borders is in defining, temporarily and dynamically rather than eternally and fixedly, political space, playing institutional and normative roles that help to limit and restrict the politically mute voice of violence and that allows individuals to build, through their plurality, a distinctive political community. This makes them ethically significant. It is not about values being territorially specific – unique to Asia, for example – it is about the need for values to gain purchase and have effect within a political context and that means within a communal context. The value of borders may well be in the bordering of values, but not in an essentialist way that assumes community is somehow fixed and immune from alteration through interaction with outsiders. The dynamism, unpredictability and immanent potential for change that characterises political action makes all such universal and total claims hubristic. The corkscrewing trajectory of globalisation and the shock of 9/11 are two examples of this unpredictability that highlight the need for a politics that does not rely on universal blueprints for its normative appeal and ethical defence. 'Ruling' has not served us well as a way to respond to rapid change and unexpected and violent challenges. A politics of engagement, debate and open-minded toleration, as well as bold and clear-sighted resistance to the intolerable, offers an alternative that is more open to the significance of difference in human life and more realistic about the role and nature of basic social institutions. It is also superior in an ethical understanding of the role of territorial borders, those deeply enduring yet strangely neglected lines on the map that are so much more than just a part of the material fixtures and fittings of international politics.

5
Shifting Lines in the Sand

Introduction

The riddle of territorial borders remains. Their symbolic power continues to be immense – symbolic of sovereignty, of nationalism, of power and authority. The disputes that accompany their location on the map have created some of the world's most enduring conflicts, in Kashmir, Korea and 'Kurdistan', for the sake of alliterative example. Their manifest artificiality – most striking in the bold, ruled lines characteristic of certain African and Middle Eastern borders – sits ill at ease alongside various insistences on the 'naturalness' of other borders, necessitated by the unbreakable connection of a certain group of people to a certain piece of land. Their role in defining classic military security questions has been augmented by issues of societal security, and policy matters such as immigration control and the future of the system governing claims to political asylum.[1] Strengthening border controls has also been part of the US government's response to 9/11. This has included a narrowing of the visa waiver scheme on foreign nationals travelling to the United States alongside the imposition of other more stringent and intrusive immigration controls, such as routine finger-printing, and the searching and interviewing of passengers. Holding the line against terrorism is taking place along the points of entry to sovereign territory, at the territorial border.

Asserting authority over those entering and leaving the state at the border has been accompanied, though, by the continuing onrush of the de-bordering of other aspects of human activity. Global communications and interconnectivity draw not so much a bayonet through the sand to mark those who are within from those without, but a fibre-optic cable or the even less tangible beam of satellite communications to link and join those on the privileged side of the 'digital divide'. There seems little prospect of human beings moving beyond borders of one sort or another and given the depth of the sediment accumulated around territorial borders and the enduring appeal of the state as a political project, that some of those borders will be territorial and that these will be used as the basis for the separation of political authority also seem inescapable.

This is, though, now a commonplace of the political geographic literature.[2] What this book has tried to explore is whether this might, to put it simply, actually be a good thing. Our task has been to see if geographical thinking about territorial borders can be augmented and moved forward by bringing to bear some of the insights of international political theory, especially where this has taken a strongly normative and ethical turn. Clearly, the book has tried to make a case for the benefits of such an approach and to argue that a recognition of the social construction of territorial borders as institutions of international politics must also result in ethical enquiry, as well as enquiry into the social structures of power and authority that brought about, sustain and legitimise the territorial demarcation of political space. The critical perspective that has arisen from these enquiries has stressed the power-based aspects of territorial borders; the way that the division of political space has resulted in repressive, violent and discriminatory practice.[3] The record of recent history in relation to areas where territorial border disputes have become, or have long been, central has understandably influenced this agenda. The 1990s experience of the resurgence of ethno-nationalist violence in the Balkans; the intensification of violence in the Israel–Palestine dispute over the last 7 or 8 years and the irresolvability of territorial questions there; the failure of the Cypriot unification referendum; and the teetering on the brink of Kashmir help to fuel a sense of cynicism and despair about progress in the territorial affairs of some of the world's more troubled places.[4]

One danger of this approach, though, is to see territorial borders, especially when they are subsumed within a dominant Westphalian notion of sovereignty, as being almost exclusively top–down creations – a device invented and imposed by elites for their own nefarious purposes; creating division, enmity, difference and separation in opposition to some sort of inherent human commonality or uniformity. The idea of a world society of human individuals, united by something more than biological commonality that can provide the basis for ethical universalism, is a powerful one, with far-reaching implications for territorial borders, as discussed in Chapter 3. This reinforces the sense of territorial borders as imposition, as artificial creators of separate identities. The liberalism that we have also traced in the construction of the idea of territorial borders makes the case weightier still. Before diversity there is unity, and diversity is a created overlay that can be peeled back and stripped away in the search for foundations or, less philosophically, can be changed and amended in order to retain the desirable parts of such diversity whilst containing the undesirable. Sectarianism, bigotry, racism, homophobia, misogyny and so on can be excised; cultural richness, mutual understanding and progress through shared experience and dialogue can be preserved.[5]

Chapter 4's argument rests in important ways on a challenge to this idea, though, asserting the need to put the horse of diversity back in front of the cart of territorial borders, or at least, and to mix metaphors, to offer greater recognition of the equality of the two partners in the relationship. Drawing on Arendt offers one way, I think a useful way, of giving this move intellectual momentum and, in particular, kick-starting ethical enquiry. The emphasis Arendt lays on the fundamental importance of plurality to the human condition reminds us forcefully that diversity in human affairs can be seen as more than the product of socialisation, more than an overlay on top of human uniformity. Equally, her discussion of the necessity of community to human fulfilment and meaningfulness, and the role of political action in this regard balances the tendency to portray political communities in top–down, power-based ways. The inescapability of bordering, and the importance of territorial bordering, that we can read from Arendt's recognition of the importance of limits in politics, returns territorial borders to the political world, as the social constructivist turn requires, but in a novel way. Ethical defensibility becomes a real prospect as we treat these social practices with due seriousness, rather than as adjuncts of sovereignty, of international order or of human rights. We need territorial borders and we should have and defend territorial borders because they are part of the ways in which human beings confer meaning on their lives through conferring recognition upon one another as related, as connected, as special and as fellow members of something that is special, because it is separate.

This does not have to be territorially bound. The idea of an international in-between is one that I have argued for elsewhere, and the globalisation of civil society, and of some pretty uncivil societies, is not a process or project that is being rejected here.[6] A die-in-the-ditch defence of Westphalian territoriality is not what has been on offer. But neither is an assumption that the passing of the Westphalian order, if that is what we are seeing, brings to an end the debates about the ethics of territorial borders. A non-sovereign or semi-sovereign world, or whatever other future constitutive normative structure for international, or global, politics emerges, will retain territorial borders of some sort or another because this seems to be a part of the way that human societies work and it has made a major contribution to the ideas that we have about belonging, about ethics, and about how we gain a sense of place in the world, enabling us to interact with other human beings on the basis of trust, of promising and forgiveness.

This need not always be on the basis of inclusion. As Barry Buzan points out in his analysis of English school theory, there is a tendency to equate 'society' and 'community' with 'niceness'.[7] This, however, need not be the case, as Buzan notes, and there is plenty of social activity that can be exclusive. Hatred is just as strong a basis for social action as love, and the mechanisms for creating social structures can be coercion and instrumental calculation, as well as shared identity.[8] The possibility, indeed likelihood, of societies looking to close themselves off from others, to preserve a sense of unique identity through exclusion, through the heightening of difference and through the rejection of engagement, has to be possible within our schema for ethical thinking and, as Chapter 4 suggests, to be respected, at least up to a point.

Territorial borders have played an important role in this kind of exclusionary practice in the past, and the logic of *modus vivendi* that informs the classical pluralism of the English school provides a contingent ethical justification that retains great appeal in many parts of the world, or at least amongst the political elites of many of the world's states, which is not necessarily the same thing. This, however, relies on the subsuming of territorial borders within a system constituted by the norm of sovereignty and there seems no good enough empirical evidence or ethical argument to accept that this connection has to be accepted. Treating territorial borders as ethically significant practices in and of themselves allows for a richer connection between territorial bordering and human plurality and communal diversity to be explored, with the role of territorial borders as a part of this ethically desirable process being recognised.

Shifting the lines on the map may be the activity that has received the majority of attention in the Westphalian era and, since 1945, has been looked upon with the gravest suspicion.[9] However, the need to divide territorially has been seen as a bureaucratic or functional matter, rather than one for ethical debate, because of the perception of the overriding imperative to protect the basis of order.[10] Debates over the rights and, more often, the wrongs of territorial bordering have been dominated by the concern for order between states, even when overlaid with a gloss of the language of national self-determination and an appeal to the ethical ideals of freedom, liberty, equality, justice and so on.[11]

Therefore, we need to recognise the need to engage with what we may regard as anti-social communities or activities, with efforts to resist engagement and to appeal to a past that may, in the eyes of the teleologically inclined, be a Canute-like effort to hold back the tide of progress, history, capitalism, technology or whatever other irresistible material force is seen to be driving history. This engagement may involve accepting the creation of metaphorical, or possibly even real, fences between communities, acknowledging one another as human beings, and acknowledging plurality in the process, whilst respecting a community's decisions to be different, to work out the social needs of their society in alternative ways. Holding open the possibility for change, recognising the need for politics as a popular, unpredictable and potentially radically participatory activity and seeing it as vital to the meaning of human lives are universal, though. Intolerance, a refusal to reciprocate recognition of humanity through plurality, especially where violent and aimed at the destruction of communal identities, becomes intolerable. This is more than an agreement to disagree, it is an agreement to commit to a more human, because more diverse, world and that also means a world in which territorial borders, alongside other kinds of divides and distinctions, will need to persist.

The issue of the end of the Westphalian era raises the question of the future of territorial borders and the kinds of ethical debates that are likely to take place. If the characterisation of the system as more 'Westfailure',[12] than Westphalia, has mileage, then these issues are not simply of interest to academics, but may have potentially significant knock-on consequences for policy debates about how the role and status of territorial borders, and, in some cases, their location on the map, should be addressed. It is to these issues that we turn in this final chapter and in particular whether we can speculate about the role that territorial borders ought to play in a more just world. As the preceding arguments have hopefully made clear, this is not about proposing models for an ideal world, some sort of post-Westphalian reprise of the eighteenth-century fashion for perpetual peace schemes.[13] Instead, it is about interrogating the immanent potential in existing practice, thinking about those trends at work in contemporary international politics, exploring how actors are addressing current challenges. A chapter such as this, indeed a book such as this, which has operated principally at the level of the abstract, can only hope to rough out an agenda for enquiry along these lines, rather than set out to fulfil it. The importance of context, the needs of the specific communities and the roles that territorial borders play in their discourse, the dangers of hubris and the imponderables of the future ensure that prediction is well beyond what is possible here.

Instead, what we can hope to try and do is point out ways in which the kind of ethical agenda mapped out here could, or should, influence thinking in political geography, international political theory and debates about globalisation. It would be unwise to attempt to do this on the basis of these distinctions, though, as the fields are too big, and the mastery of their literatures unavailable, to sustain authoritative statements. Instead, certain key themes have emerged from this enquiry that point to how an ethical take on territorial borders can make a contribution. These themes include the idea of 'the territorial trap', and the danger of creating a different version of that trap; the relationship between world society and the states-system under conditions of globalisation; and the role of violence in a world where fear of terrorism and a desire to respond effectively to human catastrophes have created major challenges for established ways of compartmentalising and containing violence.

Revisiting and recreating the territorial trap

The ability of international relations to resist the lure of the 'territorial trap', the static and materialist portrayal of territory that reifies and de-politicises the idea, has been significant but, surely, can no longer be justifiable. Theories of international relations that continue to take for granted the pre-eminence of the state as an actor and to homogenise in an ahistorical fashion the idea of the state as an actor are in danger of losing analytical purchase. They have to take seriously the arguments from political geographers, social constructivists and others that the nature and role of territory, including the lines that enclose territory, are dynamic. The idea of states as 'like units', and that pretty much any sort of independent political community can be treated as analogous to a state, brings theoretical parsimony, rigour and clarity, but at too high a cost.[14]

As this argument has tried to show, and in this it is in the mainstream of post-positivist international political theorising, the ideational aspects of the state, in this case its territorial borders, are more significant than any material bases to which appeals can be made.[15] As a social phenomenon, dynamism is inherent and thus the potential for change is unavoidably immanent. Unless we can make some kind of panglossian, and utterly implausible, argument that we live in the best of all possible worlds, then the ethical question becomes unavoidable and the need for a normative dimension to theory inescapable. As we have seen, issues of terrorism and humanitarian intervention, amongst others, have been used in international relations theory to launch a critical assault on the territorial trap, although mainly indirectly through seeing this as a part of the problem we face in addressing these questions adequately because of the restrictions, tensions and obstructions that the Westphalian notion of sovereignty produces.

However, this has the potential to re-create a different sort of territorial trap and there is a need to guard against this. In this trap the negative consequences associated with the dominant conceptualisation of territory become reified, generating a reverse of the current trap. The idea of the bordering of territory becomes associated with repression, violence, anti-politics and the construction of notions of identity, belonging and authority that are driven by elites whose overriding concern is the legitimation of their own power.[16] As a result, territorialisation becomes part of imperial, hegemonic or other projects that are perceived and portrayed as at odds with ethically far more desirable outcomes such as equality, freedom or justice. The use of these terms by political leaders, for example the repeated use of phrases such as 'freedom-loving peoples everywhere' by President George W. Bush, should be regarded with scepticism bordering on cynicism. This is rhetorical window-dressing to fool the gullible and to disguise 'real' motivations that are connected to some sort of power-political hidden agenda.

This is not to suggest that we suspend disbelief in relation to what political leaders tell us, or that we accept at face value the intellectual coherence of arguments that frequently depend on all sorts of doubtful conflations, confused ethical schemas or dubious empirical premises. Nevertheless, in a world of our making, to borrow Nicholas Onuf's book title that so helpfully sums up one of constructivism's core tenets, there are several reasons for resisting the lure of cynicism, even when political leaders may appear to do everything to encourage it.

The first of these is the intellectual point that for constructivists words must matter and have to be taken seriously. This may be to varying degrees and in different ways, with, for example, the sort of constructivism that Onuf or Kratochwil are associated with, with its debts to Wittgenstein, placing greater emphasis on language than Wendt's version, with its basis in symbolic interactionist sociology.[17] Nevertheless, the discursive framing of events, ideas, facts and theories plays an important role in the significance they gain for political action. The political need to make arguments that appeal to major ethical ideas in defence of political action matters as a result because it opens the door to ethical debate in political affairs and provides mechanisms and structures through which political actors can be held to account. These mechanisms and structures may be weaker than many would like, and there are doubtless instances where 'rhetorical window dressing' is a perfectly accurate label, but the immanent potential for ethical engagement is held open.

Closing this window, at least in relation to thinking about territorial borders and territoriality more generally, by overemphasising the power-political, repressive and hegemonic aspects of the Westphalian system is a mistake. Seeing in this the principal, let alone the only, way in which territorial borders can operate in international politics abandons the claim to dynamism and immanence in social practice that is one of constructivism's core claims. It re-creates a territorial trap by denying the immanent potential for change that is present in all social practices, such as territorial bordering, and seeks to deny the role of separation in ethical thinking. Even if the argument presented here for seeing human plurality as being of fundamental significance to ethics because of its centrality to the human condition has not been persuasive, the endurance and ubiquity of the practice of dividing political communities, political authority and political rights and obligations through the use of territorial borders should give serious pause for thought before dismissing territorial borders as ethically contingent, ethically null or ethically undesirable in and of themselves. Our critique of the 'Westfailure' system, and its many egregious ethical shortcomings, should not result in an over hasty dismissal of a fundamentally important social practice.

The second reason for resisting cynicism is more pragmatic, although it, too, has roots in the kind of political theory that this book has drawn on and which can be found in other normatively engaged theories that emphasise discourse, such as Andrew Linklater's version of critical theory.[18] Cynicism is corrosive of the kind of public life, of the kind of political participation that these theories propose and endorse. The virtues of a participatory politics cannot take place under conditions of general cynicism. Whilst this is hardly the place to engage in a serious analysis of declining political participation across the industrialised world, at least in the party political process, it is worth noting this problem. The hopes of advocates of new social movements and the idea of a nascent global civil society that alternative channels of political participation and communication are being opened is one bright spot.[19] However, such groups, networks and forms of politics can fall prey to the same cynical charges, too. The mantra of 'might makes right', or, to take the classical version, 'the strong do what they can and the weak suffer what they must',[20] and, by extension, notions of right have no independent value is a flawed one. It falls prey to the criticism of 'yardstick' ethics discussed in Chapter 2 and treats as axiomatic the idea that where there is power there can be no ethics, whereas the argument put forward in this book has been supportive of the idea that might and right are engaged in a complicated, but symbiotic, relationship. Notions of power and ethics belong together, not apart, and stable and durable political systems derive these characteristics not simply from coercive muscle or instrumental calculation, but from an ability to tap into ethical ideas that are an important part of social cohesion. Where people believe in the ability or potential of their political communities and systems of governance to deliver some passable facsimile of a good life, this should be respected, not dismissed as the result of false consciousness, the machinations of power holders or mass brainwashing through education and other enculturing experiences, as opposed to some extra-political notion of ethical perfection.

The other territorial trap that potentially lies in wait, although the argument in this book has been that this is a less likely outcome, is to dismiss the relevance of territory and territorial borders in the face of globalisation. Territorial borders as hangovers from a Westphalian system of declining, and ultimately doomed, significance makes the same kind of assumptions about their material and immutable nature as the original version of the trap. Equally, the assumption that because the current construction of territorial borders leaves little room for independent ethical value it is impossible for such value to be a part of a de-bordered or, more plausibly, re-bordered future does not automatically follow. In exploring the shift to a post-Westphalian political system there is a need to carry through those aspects of the existing system that preserve, protect and encourage engagement with and involvement in politics as part of the process of generating ethical systems and schemas. As noted, this needs to involve issues of exclusion and separation as well as inclusion and unity. For some the levels of separation and exclusion will be higher than for others. These cannot be absolute, because of the ethical imperatives behind the possibility of change and against a violent and intolerant rejection of the possibility of engagement, but they may be quite extensive. Territorial separations through borders are a conceivable part of this, indeed, given the endurance of this sort of separating device, a likely part. Globalisation does not mean, and should not mean, the end of territorial borders.

Globalisation, world society and the states-system

This brings us to the second theme of this concluding chapter, the relationship between world society and the states-system. Given the

use of the English school as a starting point and foil for understanding this relationship, it is unsurprising that it is the potential of
this theoretical approach that is emphasised here. In particular, Barry
Buzan's reformulation of the English school's understanding of
world society and his effort to clarify and make more rigorous the
structure of theory has been influential in the argument here.
Buzan's analysis self-consciously focuses on the structural level,
though, and although sensitive to the importance of the normative
space that the English school has always held open, and which has
helped to distinguish this approach from more 'hard nosed' and
morally sceptical realist approaches, it is not an aspect that receives a
great deal of attention in his study.[21]

In particular, Buzan's decision to separate analytically the states-
system from world society, even when the states-system is characterised by a strongly cosmopolitan ethical sense as with the kind of
confederative system advocated in Kant's Perpetual Peace, plays well
with the ethical argument developed here.[22] Thus, I too have argued
for a conception of world society that is populated by non-state
actors, rather than seeing it as a category where an international
society of states is augmented by individuals and non-state actors.[23]
Equally, and as I have argued elsewhere, Buzan recognises that the
cosmopolitanism that is usually associated with the notion of world
society in English school theory should not be taken for granted,
either, and the possibility for a pluralist world society is one that has
to be taken seriously.[24] Indeed, a pluralist world society may well be
a more plausible outcome of the globalisation processes that are
making non-state actors of various kinds more significant. This,
however, is an empirical judgement, not a normative one, and
English school theorists need to think through seriously the ethical
arguments surrounding a pluralist world society. The argument here,
of course, is that a pluralist world society is ethically desirable, that
the cosmopolitanism that has been taken for granted in relation to
world society in some English school thinking – that which Buzan
labels the 'Vincentian' trend, in recognition of John Vincent's influence – is misplaced.[25]

As a part of this ethical exploration of world society, though, there
is a need to explore the role that territorial borders might play in
world society and the ethical implications of this. For example, this
book has argued strongly for the need to explore the ethics of territorial

borders but has nevertheless tended to see these as being primarily in terms of delimiting political communities making some claim to autonomy. In the Westphalian system this has become synonymous with states, part of the reason for the lack of ethical investigation into territorial borders, because such work has been focused on sovereignty and its consequences. However, if territorially based claims to separation and difference are to be supported as ethically desirable it becomes necessary to see whether, and if so, how, this can work in world society without producing units that become functionally undifferentiated from states, and thus move from a world society sphere to the states-system. Of course, this may prove to be impossible: the claim to 'like unit' status for almost any sort of autonomous political community irrespective of its constitutive structure, mode of coherence or self-understanding, may prove to be analytically defensible, rather than misleading oversimplification.[26] However, the argument in this book points in a different direction.

We have accepted the force of the challenge represented by globalisation, in terms of altering the structure of international politics, undermining the previously overwhelming importance of the states-system. Hedley Bull's argument of the late 1970s that the existence of states is the fundamental ontological fact of international politics cannot remain unamended.[27] However, the non-state members of world society are not all 'global' in the sense that they appeal to some sort of universalistic conception of the nature of their activity. Some, of course, are, and these are perhaps the easiest to accommodate within world society as usually conceived because of the cosmopolitan ethical bias that often influences such work. Thus environmentalists, human rights organisations, capitalists, drugs traffickers and people traders can all plausibly be said to operate with a global frame of reference, even if the activities of any one organisation may be geographically focused and specific.[28] There is nothing in principle that prevents an environmental group that concentrates its work on the Amazon rainforest from bringing its attention to bear, within a largely unchanged intellectual framework, upon the problems of retreating glaciers in the Himalayas or the declining fish stocks of the North Atlantic. Those specialising in the shipment of women from southeast Asia to the brothels of North America could also probably just as easily turn their hands to moving cocaine from South America to Western Europe, although the effort of gaining a foothold in that activity is likely to be a great deal higher, and a great deal bloodier, than for an environmental organisation looking to take on a different issue.

Non-state actors whose operations are self-consciously and necessarily geographically limited present something more of a challenge, though. Buzan deploys the idea of regionalism as a way to address this, which works well in the context of the structural theoretical level at which he is working.[29] As an explanatory tool, this is fine. However, from an ethical perspective, things are perhaps less straightforward because the justification of the regional, or narrower, boundary becomes more complicated. Non-state actors using global space for territorially specific and exclusionary practices is, nevertheless, not analytically incoherent. The idea of a 'digital umma' – a virtual Islamic community – fulfils the second of these criteria, through being exclusionary, but perhaps not the first, because whilst the idea of the umma may be limited to followers of Islam, it is not territorially specific, although, of course, specific places may play a special role in the life of that community, most obviously the holy sites of Mecca, Medina and Jerusalem.[30]

It is perhaps in diasporas that we find a contemporary example of a territorially specific and exclusionary non-state actor. This territorial specificity is not the specificity of residence, of course, but there frequently is a specificity of political focus, a sense of belonging and of being connected to a specific place, and a shared belief in the obligations to that place, too, even if these have to be carried out remotely. Political lobbying of the state of residence by diasporas on behalf of or in the interest of the 'homeland' is nothing new, and neither is the creation of concentrations of people sharing a diasporic identity in their countries of residence. The idea of 'Chinatown', 'little Naples', 'little Karachi', 'little Athens' or whatever is familiar to us all.

However, the development of technology and the growing mechanisms for bringing influence to bear remotely has the potential to make diasporas more important. On the one hand, their size is likely to grow as migration increases, raising concerns in some states about their ability to cope with large population influxes and the social consequences that arise. The traditional practice of remitting money back to family in the 'homeland' and the growing opportunity for economically active and successful diaspora members to re-invest in the 'homeland' as the global economy is freed also bring influence.

Political engagement and support for specific causes is far easier with digital communications, and the willingness and ability of diasporas to play a part in the politics of states appears to be increasing.[31]

This can cause political problems, undoubtedly, and raises challenges to the cultural predilections and settled practices of states that receive migrant populations. However, this may also be an example of the potentially ethically desirable role of territorial borders, even in a world society context. The presence of these kinds of communities reiterates the plurality of humanity and reminds us of the dynamism of politics. The engagement that takes place can help foster mutual understanding and respect. Sometimes it generates violence, hostility and intolerance, too, but that is a part of the process, and the idea of diasporic communities as 'closed' or 'separate' within the state where they have come to settle serves just as well as a mirror of the closure and separation of the 'host' society in many instances, reminding us of the need for and desirability of a degree of separation, of a mechanism for preserving difference as a part of the way that we constitute ourselves as human beings through engagement with, and differentiation from, others.

The limits we have sought to place on the ethical defensibility of territorial borders apply with just as much force in world society as they do in international society, and the idea of toleration can be thought through in essentially the same way. What this move opens up, though, is the idea of the ethical defensibility of seeking in world society a place in which to hide from globalisation, the opposite of the usual explorations. Seeking, through non-state actors, through digital communications and through the use of transnational political mechanisms, to create some sort of space, linked to territory but without aiming at sovereignty, can preserve and nurture plurality. A closing off of a group, whether in its entirety or in some aspects of its ethical life, from involvement with others, on a tolerant and non-absolute basis that does not attempt to deny the possibility of change, can be an ethically defensible response. For some, it may be an ethically desirable response, too, as they try to find ways to resist the undermining of what are regarded as vital and viable ethical schemas from the onslaught of capitalist consumerism and particularistic conceptions of ostensibly universal values such as 'freedom' or 'liberty' marketed as though they could only mean one thing.

These brief comments cannot do much more than open this line of enquiry, though. One conclusion that can be drawn, however, is that the English school's traditional pluralist stance, of a defence of the sovereign states-system the norm of non-intervention, appears increasingly unsustainable.

Territorial borders and violence

The strongest defence of the Westphalian border lies in its role in the nexus of rules and norms of interstate behaviour that aim to restrain the use of violence in international relations. However, the challenges of humanitarian intervention and transnational terrorism seem poorly dealt with by this line of argument, requiring anguished, and ineffectual, by-standing in the case of the former and distorting in the case of the latter so that it can be addressed within an interstate framework. The defence that is offered tends to be one of fear at what might happen if the rules are loosened so that the international community (of states) might be better able to deal with what Mary Kaldor labelled 'new wars' – the kind of conflicts fought by semi-organised, irregular forces fighting often brutally violent campaigns generally aimed at civilian populations and with a high element of criminality to go alongside any political objectives. The fear of abuse of relaxed rules by the powerful to pursue expansionary or hegemonic wars; the fear of the opening of 'domestic' politics to violent intrusion by outsiders allowing cultural and religious divisions contained within the Westphalian structure to once again be a *causus belli*; the fear of a slippery slope to the Hobbesian abyss of the war of all against all motivates this defence.[32]

These are powerful arguments, and they cannot be wished away or easily dismissed. Even efforts to re-think sovereignty in order to allow for a limited right to humanitarian intervention need to take these things into account in order to avoid a significantly more violent world. A good example is the way the ICISS used the idea of criteria derived from Just War theory to restrain some of the potential consequences of their argument for re-thinking sovereignty as a 'responsibility to protect', a responsibility that passes across state borders if a state's government proves either unwilling or unable to fulfil this responsibility.[33] The Commission's argument for a cosmopolitan ethical imperative behind such a responsibility needed to be tempered to be both politically palatable and also in recognition of the ethical calamity that war generally represents and the strengths of the existing system of restraints.

However, the argument here has been that such a system can demand that we tolerate the intolerable; or, more precisely, given the effort to make toleration more than forbearance, that we forbear the intolerable. Terrorism, too, poses ethical challenges, as well as practical ones, because of the frequent difficulty in effectively tying the operations of a terrorist organisation to a state government, bringing that government within the traditional targeting mechanisms of international politics. The contrasting fortunes of the Bush administration in garnering international support for its military operations against Afghanistan and Iraq is a case in point. The ethical need to effectively address indiscriminate, murderous and wholly intentional violence is beyond doubt, but the disassociation between such violence and a political agenda on the part of terrorist organisations that is comprehensible within a states-systemic context makes appealing to traditional state-systemic ethical ideas much more difficult.

Territorial borders would thus seem to be in trouble here. However, the way that such an understanding relies on a contingent ascription of ethical value may help explain this cause of trouble and give us some reason to see territorial borders in a different light that makes their role in thinking about this kind of violence more positive. In particular, the idea of territorial borders as ethically valuable because of the way that they can act as limits in politics is important here, and the role that Arendt saw for them in helping to disrupt and disturb totalitarian political projects.[34] The ability to root resistance to projects that aim at violently crushing diversity and imposing monolithic notions of 'truth' through the terror of loneliness and the politically mute voice of violence is one important aspect of this. Knowing who we are, having some ability to engage in a trusting relationship with those people with whom we share our lives and with whom we share political involvement offers a way to resist the impact of terror in disrupting these bases of political community.

The division of political authority is another element, and one that the Westphalian notion of territorial borders puts at the centre of its argument. However, the turn taken in this book seeks to place that division in a different context. Instead of an appeal to sovereignty, there is an appeal to the central role of territorial division in the fundamental idea of individual plurality and the pluralism of political community. The need for mechanisms for enabling inclusion can be met in part through territorial division and bordering, encouraging the engagement with and belonging to political community that may counter an alienation that is conducive to violence. Dividing and bordering political authority also helps in part with the challenge faced by ideas such as cosmopolitan democracy and global citizenship, which is to enable effective accountability. Holding political authority to account for its use of violence is one of the key political problems that any political system needs to address. Whilst hopes that democracies will be more peaceable because the population, who bear the cost of war, will be more reluctant to fight than their leadership may be somewhat utopian, the need for accountability remains.[35]

None of this, though, is likely to see an end to political violence and war and the consequent need to engage in ethical thinking about how, why, when and in what ways organised political violence can and even should be used.[36] Simple ethical imperatives, such as 'thou shalt not kill', have the benefit of clarity but they are not appropriate to a political ethics that has to work from what is, seeking the immanent potential within existing practice and not falling victim to the tendency to separate politics and ethics into different realms. Therefore, territorial borders may well endure as 'trip wires', marking the places where, historically, conflict is most likely to happen, and thus the places where political vigilance and engagement is most necessary. In places where diversity is at its greatest the protection and maintenance of a common understanding based on the idea of the border as a fence may be the best that can be hoped for. However, thinking about them as possessing ethical value also marks them out as places of opportunity for engagement, for dialogue and discourse about ways in which political communities can develop levels of trust and a meaningful notion of toleration that goes beyond forbearance. This speaks to the tradition in political geography that stresses the idea of border zones, rather than lines, and picks out the distinctiveness of such zones from metropolitan cores, helping remind us of the need to recall the different ways in which borders have been conceptualised.[37]

Nevertheless, the challenge of de-territorialised, transnational terrorism that appeals to a political agenda that sits uneasily within a Westphalian conception of the role of territory is one of the hardest challenges that we face in international politics. Utilising ethical ideas to condemn terrorist attacks is straightforward, but the social, political and economic circumstances that lie behind the perpetration of such violence are unlikely to be so easily condemned. This is not to seek to excuse such violence, or to seek some kind of ethical amelioration for those who resort to these tactics. Instead, though, there is a requirement that we explore the ethical traditions that are used, and abused, in offering justification but not always in the anticipation that this will result in reconciliation, compromise or a shared recognition of ethical universals arising from traditions that may share very different 'source stories'. Sometimes we will want, and it will be right, to put up barriers, metaphysical and metaphorical and not only territorial, and to decide on a postponement, perhaps for a long time, of discussion of some questions, so long as they do not fall outside the limits of toleration. But, when faced by the intolerable, we may have to fight.

Conclusion

The territorial borders of the world are amongst the most fundamental institutions of international politics, shaping the lives of everyone who lives on the planet to some extent and, in the case of those made refugees or who find themselves fighting wars over borders or living near borders being fought over, they can be a matter of life and death. Drawing lines in the sand and across the maps is thus a political activity of the utmost significance, dividing communities, families and nations and laying the basis for new efforts at collective identity formation. Where to locate those lines has been the cause of wars and, perhaps in a few cases, the cause of peace, too, as mechanisms have been found to separate those who no longer wish to share a state, such as Czechoslovakia's 'velvet divorce'. That there will be lines and that they will serve as mechanisms of division, has generally been taken for granted, and certainly this has been a central part of the idea of the Westphalian system. The shifting sands of our title have been literal in some cases, but certainly a metaphor that retains a powerful physical and material element. As the tide of a state's power has ebbed and flowed then so too, frequently, has the location of its territorial borders expanded and contracted to take in a greater or lesser share of the earth's surface.

The metaphor we have mainly been concerned with in this book, though, is a more distant one. The shifting sands have been more intellectual, in terms of the academic critiques coming from political geography and international political theory that have underpinned the argument that has been developed. Equally, the shifting sands of the organisational framework of international politics – the social practices and structures of globalization – are at some distance to the traditional notion of defining and specifying territorial borders, raising questions, as they do, about not just the location of borders, but their role, too. It is these shifts that necessitate a re-examination of the ethics of territorial borders, and a re-examination that treats them as significant in and of themselves, rather than as adjuncts of other ideas, such as sovereignty or order.

The argument that I have tried to develop offers one version of such an enquiry, but it would be indefensible to pretend that it is the only such enquiry that can be mounted. A more ethically cosmopol- itan, and probably liberal, account could be developed, too. Equally, a better defence of the Westphalian conception than that currently available could be put forward. Thus, this can not stand as a last word on the subject of the ethics of territorial borders but it will, hopefully, stand as some sort of way station on the way to a richer, more focused and clearer-sighted debate about the ethics of these vitally important features of our political world.

Notes

1 Introduction

1. E.g. Gearóid Ó Thuathail (1996), *Critical Geopolitics*, London: Routledge. Chris Brown (2002), *Sovereignty, Rights and Justice: International Political Theory Today*, Cambridge: Polity, pp. 179–85. David Newman and Anssi Paasi (1998), 'Fences and Neighbours in the Postmodern World: Boundary Narratives in Political Geography', *Progress in Human Geography* 22 (2).
2. Kenichi Ohmae (1991), *The Borderless World: Power and Strategy in the Interlinked Economy*, London: Fontana. Kenichi Ohmae (1995), *The End of the Nation State: The Rise of Regional Economies*, London: HarperCollins. Kenichi Ohmae (2001), *The Invisible Continent: Four Strategic Imperatives of the New Economy*, London: Nicholas Brealey.
3. The term is taken from Jan Aart Scholte (2000), *Globalization: A Critical Introduction*, Basingstoke: Palgrave.
4. E.g. 'Introduction' in Nigel Dower and John Williams (eds) (2002), *Global Citizenship: A Critical Reader*, Edinburgh: Edinburgh University Press.
5. Derek Heater (1996), *World Citizenship and Government: Cosmopolitan Ideas in the History of Western Political Thought*, Basingstoke: Macmillan.
6. Nigel Dower (2002), 'Global Ethics and Global Citizenship', in Dower and Williams (eds), *Global Citizenship*.
7. Dower and Williams, 'Introduction', in Dower and Williams (eds), *Global Citizenship*, p. 7.
8. For a useful, and critical, summary of these arguments see Chris Brown (2001), 'Cosmopolitanism, World Citizenship and Global Civil Society', in Simon Caney and Peter Jones (eds), *Human Rights and Cultural Diversity*, London: Frank Cass.
9. For an interesting discussion of the politics of such groups see Anthony F. Lang, Jr (2005), 'Governance and Political Action: Hannah Arendt on Global Political Protest', in Anthony F. Lang, Jr and John Williams (eds), *Hannah Arendt and International Relations: Readings Across the Lines*, New York: Palgrave.
10. A classic account of this 'network' approach is offered by Manuel Castells (1996/7), *The Information Age: Economy, Society and Culture*, Oxford: Blackwell.
11. An excellent summary is offered by Scholte, *Globalization* especially Section 1.
12. E.g. Susan Strange (1999), 'The Westfailure System', *Review of International Studies*, 25 (3). Brown, *Sovereignty, Rights and Justice*, pp. 231–48.
13. There are a large number of accounts of the dissolution of the SFRY and its aftermath, reaching varying conclusions about the reasons for the

catastrophic outcome of the process, and where blame should be apportioned. See James Gow (1997), *Triumph of the Lack of Will: International Diplomacy and the Yugoslav War*, London: Hurst. James Gow (2003), *The Serbian War Project and its Adversaries: A Strategy of War Crimes*, London: Hurst. David Campbell (1998), *National Deconstruction: Violence, Identity and Justice in Bosnia*, Minneapolis: University of Minnesota Press. Thomas Cushman and Stjepan G. Mestrovic (eds) (1996), *This Time We Knew: Western Responses to Genocide in Bosnia*, New York: New York University Press.

14. For a sceptical view, see Paul Hirst and Graeme Thompson (1999), *Globalization in Question: The International Economy and the Possibilities of Globalization*, Cambridge: Polity. Susan Strange (1998), 'Globaloney', *Review of International Political Economy* 5.

15. E.g. John Gerard Ruggie (1998), 'Territoriality at Millennium's End', in John Gerard Ruggie, *Constructing the World Polity: Essays on International Institutionalization*, London: Routledge.

16. E.g. John Williams (2003), 'Territorial Borders, International Ethics and Political Geography: Do Good Fences Still Make Good Neighbours?', *Geopolitics* 8 (2). Jouni Häkli (2001), 'In the Territory of Knowledge: State-Centred Discourses and the Construction of Society', *Progress in Human Geography* 25 (3).

17. John Gerard Ruggie, 'What Makes the World Hang Together? Neo Utilitarianism and the Social Constructivist Challenge', *International Organization* 52 (4): 873.

18. Trying to summarise the literature on these questions in a footnote is probably pointless – it would be too long a list – but a good example of how social political processes can carry meaning for borders in a specific set of political circumstances can be found in William Walters (2002), 'De-Naturalising the Border: The Politics of Schengenland', *Environment and Planning D: Society and Space* 20 (5).

19. Probably the best known example of this move in International Relations is Alexander Wendt's highly influential version of social constructivism. See Alexander Wendt (1999), *Social Theory of International Politics*, Cambridge: Cambridge University Press.

20. E.g. Steve Smith (2000), 'International Relations: Still an American Social Science?' *British Journal of Politics and International Relations* 2 (3).

21. An early, and classic, instance of this argument is Robert O. Keohane (1988), 'International Institutions: Two Approaches', *International Studies Quarterly* 32 (4).

22. The obvious target here is neo-realism as defined in Kenneth Waltz (1979), *Theory of International Politics*, New York: Addison Wesley Longman.

23. The label 'international political theory' is borrowed from Brown, *Sovereignty, Rights and Justice*, and preferred for the reasons he gives there – that it encompasses more than alternatives like 'normative theory' and highlights the connection, and indebtedness, to political theory more traditionally understood than alternatives. Given the

reliance later in the book on elements of political theory it thus seems appropriate.

24. The classic modern account of Just War, which resists this ghettoisation, is Michael Walzer (1977/92/2002), *Just and Unjust Wars: A Theoretical Argument with Historical Illustrations*, New York: Basic Books.

25. Accounts, and rejections, of this, and other, bases for moral scepticism can be found in Mervyn Frost (1996), *Ethics in International Relations*, Cambridge: Cambridge University Press and Nigel Dower (1998), *World Ethics: The New Agenda*, Edinburgh: Edinburgh University Press.

26. E.g. Frost, *Ethics in International Relations*; Brown, *Sovereignty, Rights and Justice*; Dower, *World Ethics*.

27. Kimberley Hutchings (1999), *International Political Theory: Rethinking Ethics in a Global Era*, London: Sage.

28. Probably the best known version of this claim is Wendt's slogan that the international system is made up of 'ideas, all the way down'. Wendt, *Social Theory of International Politics*, especially Chapter 3. For another, earlier, version of this sort of claim, although here resting on an understanding of the construction of rules and rule indebted to Wittgenstein, see Nicholas Onuf (1989), *World of Our Making: Rules and Rule in Social Theory and International Relations*, Columbia, SC: University of South Carolina Press.

29. The central text of the English school, and particularly the kind of summary offered here, is Hedley Bull (1977), *The Anarchical Society: A Study of Order in World Politics*, London: Macmillan.

30. An example in which international society is portrayed as fragile is Robert H. Jackson (2000), *The Global Covenant: Human Conduct in a World of States*, Oxford: Oxford University Press. A more robust portrayal can be found in Nicholas J. Wheeler (2000), *Saving Strangers: Humanitarian Intervention in International Society*, Oxford: Oxford University Press.

31. The classic statement of the problem is Bull, *The Anarchical Society*, Chapter 4. For a critique of the way the distinction has tended to be used, see John Williams (2005), 'Pluralism, Solidarism and the Emergence of World Society in English School Theory', *International Relations* 19 (1).

32. A summary of the way that cosmopolitan theory, generally of a liberal kind, discusses borders can be found in Brown, *Sovereignty, Rights and Justice*, pp. 179–85.

33. For one set of answers to this question, see *Review of International Studies* (2000), *How Might We Live?* 26 (Special issue).

34. This develops and extends an argument in John Williams (2002), 'Territorial Borders, Toleration and the English School', *Review of International Studies* 28 (4).

35. One of the best discussions of this process in international relations remains James Mayall (1990), *Nationalism and International Society*, Cambridge: Cambridge University Press.

36. For a discussion of the role of 'holy' land in the case of Israel–Palestine, see Menachem Lorberbaum (2003), 'Making and Unmaking the Boundaries

of Holy Land' and Daniel Statman (2003), 'Man-Made Boundaries and Man-Made Holiness in the Jewish Tradition' both in Allen Buchanan and Margaret Moore (eds), *States, Nations and Borders: The Ethics of Making Boundaries*, Cambridge: Cambridge University Press.

37. E.g. David M. Smith (1999), 'Geography and Ethics: How Far Should We Go?', *Progress in Human Geography* 23 (1).

2   From material facts to social practices

1. John Gerard Ruggie (1998) 'Territoriality at Millennium's End', in John Gerard Ruggie, *Constructing the World Polity: Essays on International Institutionalization*, London: Routledge, p. 173.
2. Lord Curzon of Kedleston (1907), 'Romanes Lecture on the Subject of Frontiers', available at http://www-ibru.dur.ac.uk/docs/curzon.pdf.
3. Stephen D. Krasner (1999), *Sovereignty – Organized Hypocrisy*, Princeton, NJ: Princeton University Press. For a summary of recent writing, see David A. Lake (2003), 'The New Sovereignty in International Relations', *International Studies Review* 5 (3).
4. Barry Buzan (2004), *From International to World Society? English School Theory and the Social Structure of Globalisation*, Cambridge: Cambridge University Press.
5. E.g. Hendrik Spruyt (1994), *The Sovereign State and Its Competitors: An Analysis of Systems Change*, Princeton, NJ: Princeton University Press. Benno Teschke (2003), *The Myth of 1648: Class, Geopolitics and the Making of Modern International Relations*, London: Verso. Andreas Osiander (2001), 'Sovereignty, International Relations and the Westphalian Myth', *International Organization* 55 (2).
6. E.g. Andrew Linklater (1998), *The Transformation of Political Community: Ethical Foundations for a Post-Westphalian Era*, Cambridge: Polity. Hedley Bull (1977), *The Anarchical Society: A Study of Order in World Politics*, London: Macmillan, especially Section 3.
7. E.g. Hastings Donnan and Thomas M. Wilson (1999), *Borders: Frontiers of Identity, Nation and State*, Oxford: Berg.
8. E.g. Kenichi Ohmae (1990), *The Borderless World*, London: HarperCollins.
9. E.g. Gearóid Ó Thuathail (1996), *Critical Geopolitics: The Politics of Writing Global Space*, London: Routledge.
10. Chris Brown (1992), *International Relations Theory: New Normative Approaches*, Brighton: Harvester Wheatsheaf; Chris Brown (2002), *Sovereignty, Rights and Justice: International Political Theory Today*, Cambridge: Polity; Molly Cochran (2000), *Normative Theory in International Relations*, Cambridge: Cambridge University Press; Kimberley Hutchings (1999), *International Political Theory: Rethinking Ethics in a Global Political Era*, London: Sage; Mervyn Frost (1996), *Ethics in International Relations*, Cambridge: Cambridge University Press.
11. E.g. Friedrich Kratochwil (1989), *Rules, Norms and Decisions: On the Conditions of Practical and Legal Reasoning in International Relations and Domestic*

Affairs, Cambridge: Cambridge University Press; Steve Smith, Ken Booth and Marysia Zalewski (eds) (1996), *International Theory: Positivism and Beyond*, Cambridge: Cambridge University Press; Nicholas Onuf (1989), *World of Our Making*, Columbia, SC: University of South Carolina Press; Alexander Wendt (1999), *Social Theory of International Politics*, Cambridge: Cambridge University Press.

12. David M. Smith (2001), 'Geography and Ethics: Progress, or More of the Same?', *Progress in Human Geography* 25 (2). David M. Smith (1999), 'Geography and Ethics: How Far Should We Go?', *Progress in Human Geography* 23 (1): 123. David M. Smith (1998), 'How Far Should We Care? On the Spatial Scope of Beneficence', *Progress in Human Geography* 22 (1). Andrew Sayer and Michael Sorper (1997), 'Ethics Unbound: For a Normative Turn in Social Theory', *Environment and Planning D: Society and Space* 15 (1): 1.

13. The label is borrowed from John Gerard Ruggie (1998), 'What Makes the World Hang Together? Neo-Utilitarianism and the Social Constructivist Challenge', *International Organization* 52 (4): 873.

14. Barbara F. Walter (2003), 'Explaining the Intractability of Territorial Conflict', *International Studies Review* 5 (4).

15. Brown, *Sovereignty, Rights and Justice*, p. 39.

16. Kenneth N. Waltz (1979), *Theory of International Politics*, Reading, MA: Addison, Wesley Longman.

17. Curzon, 'Frontiers'.

18. David Newman and Anssi Paasi, 'Fences and Neighbours in the Postmodern World', *Progress in Human Geography* 22 (2): 187, emphasis in original.

19. Gerald Blake (2001), 'Borderlands Under Stress: Some Global Perspectives', in Martin Pratt and Janet Alison Brown (eds), *Borderlands Under Stress*, London: Kluwer Law International, p. 1.

20. Blake, 'Borderlands Under Stress', pp. 1–2.

21. Blake, 'Borderlands Under Stress', pp. 1–2.

22. Jan Aart Scholte (2005), *Globalization: A Critical Introduction (Second edition)*, Basingstoke: Macmillan.

23. E.g. Paul Hirst and Graeme Thompson (1999), *Globalization in Question*, Cambridge: Polity offer a sceptical account of globalization.

24. Robert H. Jackson (2000), *The Global Covenant: Human Conduct in a World of States*, Oxford: Oxford University Press, pp. 424–5.

25. Colin S. Gray (1999), 'The Future is the Past – With GPS', *Review of International Studies* 25 (Special issue).

26. Colin S. Gray (2002), 'World Politics as Usual After September 11: Realism Vindicated', in Tim Dunne and Ken Booth (eds), *Worlds in Collision: Terror and the Future of Global Order*, Basingstoke: Palgrave.

27. George W. Bush (2001), 'Address to a Joint Session of Congress and the American People', available at http://www.whitehouse.gov/news/releases/2001/09/20010920-8.html.

28. E.g. James D. Sidaway (2003), 'Sovereign Excess? Portraying Postcolonial Cityscapes', *Political Geography* 22 (2).

29. Jean Bethke Elshtain (2004), *Just War Against Terror: The Burden of American Power in a Violent World*, New York: Basic Books, pp. 46–8.

30. Elshtain, *Just War Against Terror*, p. 46.
31. Elshtain, *Just War Against Terror*, p. 46.
32. Donnan and Wilson, *Borders*, p. 4.
33. Georg Simmel, quoted in Herbert Dittgen (2000), 'The End of the Nation-State?', in Pratt and Brown (eds), *Borderlands Under Stress*, p. 53.
34. John Agnew and Stuart Corbridge (1995), *Mastering Space: Hegemony, Territory and Political Economy*, London: Routledge.
35. Elshtain, *Just War Against Terror*, especially pp. 85–98.
36. Waltz, *Theory of International Politics*.
37. Tuathail, *Critical Geopolitics*.
38. Tuathail, *Critical Geopolitics*, especially pp. 57–74.
39. David Newman (2000), 'Boundaries, Territory and Postmodernity: Towards Shared or Separate Spaces?' in Pratt and Brown (eds), *Borderlands Under Stress*.
40. Newman, 'Boundaries, Territories and Post-Modernity', p. 17. See Ohmae, *The Borderless World*; Kenichi Ohmae (1995), *The End of the Nation-State: The Rise of Regional Economies* (London: HarperCollins); Kenichi Ohmae (2001), *The Invisible Continent: Four Strategic Imperatives of the New Economy* (London: Nicholas Brealey). On the backlash, an interesting article is Vicki Birchfield (2005), 'José Bové and the Globalisation Countermovement', *Review of International Studies* 31 (3).
41. Newman and Passi, 'Fences and Neighbours in the Postmodern World' p. 189.
42. James N. Rosenau (1997), *Along the Domestic-Foreign Frontier: Exploring Governance in a Turbulent World*, Cambridge: Cambridge University Press.
43. For an account of the politics of the Democratic Republic of Congo that offers a different take on the interaction between external pressures and internal effectiveness, see Sidaway, 'Sovereign Excess.'
44. C. R. Nagel (2002), 'Geopolitics by Another Name: Immigration and the Politics of Assimilation', *Political Geography* 21 (8).
45. David Campbell (1992), *Writing Security: United States Foreign Policy and the Politics of Identity*, Manchester: Manchester University Press.
46. Michael Shapiro and Hayward Alker (1996) (eds), *Challenging Boundaries: Global Flows, Territorial Identities*, Minneapolis: University of Minnesota Press, 1996.
47. Newman and Paasi, 'Fences and Neighbours in the Postmodern World' p. 188.
48. Newman and Paasi, 'Fences and Neighbours in the Postmodern World' p. 187. For Rosenau's critique of realism and liberalism, see *Along the Domestic-Foreign Frontier*, pp. 30–32.
49. E.g. Harvey Starr and G. Dale Thomas (2005), 'The Nature of Borders and International Conflict: Revisiting Hypotheses on Territory', *International Studies Quarterly* 49 (1). Walter, 'Explaining the Intractability of Territorial Conflict'. Kalevi J. Holsti (1991), *Peace and War: Armed Conflicts and International Order, 1648–1989*, Cambridge: Cambridge University Press. John A. Vasquez (1993), *The War Puzzle*, Cambridge: Cambridge University Press.

50. E.g. R. B. J. Walker (1992), *Inside/Outside: International Relations as Political Theory*, Cambridge: Cambridge University Press.
51. E.g. Cynthia Enloe (1989), *Bananas, Beaches and Bases: Making Feminist Sense of International Politics*, London: Pandora Press. J. Ann Tickner (1992), *Gender in International Relations: Feminist Perspectives on Achieving Global Security*, New York: Columbia University Press.
52. Newman and Paasi note this metaphorical usage in general, 'Fences and Neighbours in the Postmodern World' p. 188.
53. There are many accounts of this move in international relations theory. See, for example, Jim George (1994), *Discourses of Global Politics: A Critical (re)introduction to International Relations*, Boulder: Lynne Reinner.
54. The most highly developed, although not necessarily the most persuasive, account of the ideational nature of the international system is Wendt, *Social Theory of International Politics*, especially pp. 92–138.
55. Hutchings, *International Political Theory*.
56. Ken Booth (1995), 'Human Wrongs and International Relations', *International Affairs* 71 (1).
57. E.g. Walker, *Inside/Outside*.
58. An early example of this, although from a very different perspective to Walker's, is Charles R. Beitz (1979), *Political Theory and International Relations*, Princeton: Princeton University Press.
59. 'International society' is used here in the English school sense: 'A *society of states* (or international society) exists when a group of states, conscious of certain common interests and common values, form a society in the sense that they conceive themselves to be bound by a common set of rules in their relations with one another, and share in the working of common institutions.' Bull, *The Anarchical Society*, p. 13.
60. This is a consistent theme of Amnesty International's analysis of counter-terrorism proposals in the United Kingdom. E.g. Amnesty International (2005), 'The Prevention of Terrorism Bill: A Grave Threat to Human Rights and the Rule of Law in the UK', available at http://web.amnesty.org/library/index/engeur450052005. In the United States, the American Civil Liberties Union has mounted a campaign to reform the 'Patriot Act', passed in the aftermath of 9/11 on similar grounds. See http://action.aclu.org/reformthepatriotact/.
61. Campbell, *Writing Security*.
62. The charge that a United Kingdom government dossier on Iraqi weapons of mass destruction was 'sexed up' to make the case for war more compelling was famously reported by BBC journalist Andrew Gilligan, sparking a bitter row between the UK government and the BBC, that tragically involved the suicide of Gilligan's source, Dr David Kelly, a senior Ministry of Defence (MoD) expert and former weapons inspector.
63. Tony Blair (2004), 'PM warns of continuing global terror threat', http://www.pm.gov.uk/output/Page5459.asp.
64. Brown, *International Relations Theory*.

65. E.g. Michael Walzer (1983), *Spheres of Justice: A Defence of Pluralism and Equality*, Oxford: Robertson. David Miller (1995), *On Nationality*, Oxford: Clarendon.
66. Brown, *International Relations Theory*.
67. Linklater, *The Transformation of Political Community*.
68. Frost, *Ethics in International Relations*.
69. Hutchings, *International Political Theory*, especially pp. 55–90.
70. Cochran, *Normative Theory in International Relations*, pp. 21–120.
71. Cochran, *Normative Theory*, p. 118.
72. Cochran, *Normative Theory*, pp. 173–211.
73. Cochran, *Normative Theory*, p. 255.
74. This can be a problem even for post-positivist ethical theories. Cochran, *Normative Theory*, pp. 167–70.
75. Cochran, *Normative Theory*, pp. 173–272.
76. Newman, 'Boundaries Territory and Postmodernity'.
77. Sayer and Storper, 'Ethics Unbound: For a Normative Turn in Social Theory', p. 1.
78. Smith, 'Geography and Ethics'.
79. One example of this near paranoia is Tuathail's critique of Luttwak's 'geo-economics', which he introduces by highlighting Luttwak's Transylvanian ancestry. Tuathail, *Critical Geopolitics* p. 231. See the critique of post-modern and post-structural theory's ethical failures in Sayer and Storper, 'Ethics Unbound', especially pp. 4–5.
80. E.g. Bhikhu Parekh (1999), 'Non-Ethnocentric Universalism', in Tim Dunne and Nicholas J. Wheeler (eds), *Human Rights in Global Politics*, Cambridge: Cambridge University Press, p. 150.
81. Bush, 'Address to a Joint Session of Congress and the American People'.
82. George W. Bush (2002), 'President's Remarks at the United Nations General Assembly', available at http://www.whitehouse.gov/news/releases/2002/09/20020912-1.html.
83. Hutchings, *International Political Theory*, pp. 28–54.
84. E.g. Ruggie, 'Territoriality at Millennium's End'.
85. Ruggie, 'What Makes the World Hang Together?'.
86. Sayer and Storper, 'Ethics Unbound' p. 11.
87. Newman, 'Boundaries, Territory and Postmodernity' p. 19.
88. Sayer and Storper, 'Ethics Unbound' p. 11.
89. Frost's constitutive theory has sometimes been seen as open to this charge, although he avoids it in my view. For discussions of Frost's theory, see Cochran, *Normative Theory*, pp. 78–120; Peter Sutch (2000), 'Human Rights as Settled Norms: Mervyn Frost and the Limits of Hegelian Human Rights Theory', *Review of International Studies* 26 (2); John Williams (1998), 'Mervyn Frost and the Constitution of Liberalism', *Journal of Peace Research* 35 (4).
90. Spruyt, *The Sovereign State and Its Competitors*.

91. Spruyt, *Sovereign State*.
92. Spruyt, *Sovereign State*, pp. 77–108.
93. Spruyt, *Sovereign State*, pp. 77–108.
94. Spruyt, *Sovereign State*, pp. 153–80.
95. Ruggie, 'What Makes the World Hang Together?'.
96. Martha Finnemore and Kathryn Sikkink, (1998), 'International Norm Dynamics and Political Change', *International Organization* 52 (4).
97. Recall the arguments of Blake about the requirements for 'stress free borderlands'.
98. E.g. Martin Wight (1977), *Systems of States*, Leicester: Leicester University Press, Chapter 6.
99. Nicholas J. Wheeler (2001), 'Humanitarian Vigilantes or Legal Entrepreneurs? Enforcing Human Rights in International Society', in Simon Caney and Peter Jones (eds), *Human Rights and Global Diversity*, London: Frank Cass.
100. E.g. Blair, 'Continuing Global Terror Threat'. This has, though, been something of a theme of the Blair government, led by the Prime Minister, since 9/11. John Williams with Tim Roach (2006), 'Security, Territorial Borders and British Iraq Policy: Buying a Blair Way to Heaven?', *Geopolitics* 11 (1).
101. E.g. (2003), 'Roundtable: Evaluating the Pre-Emptive Use of Force', *Ethics and International Affairs* 17 (1).
102. A target here is Wendt, *Social Theory of International Politics*. E.g. Steve Smith (2000), 'The Discipline of International Relations: Still an American Social Science?' *British Journal of Politics and International Relations* 2 (3).
103. Jackson, *Global Covenant*, pp. 44–96. Richard Little (2000), 'The English School's Contribution to the Study of International Relations', *European Journal of International Relations* 6 (3). Christian Reus-Smit (2001), 'Imagining Society: Constructivism and the English School', *The British Journal of Politics and International Relations* 4 (3).
104. Although for an important critique of this, see Buzan, *From International to World Society?*.

3   The ethical contingency of territorial borders?

1. The humanitarian intervention literature is huge, and extends into a range of fields beyond international relations, including international law and moral philosophy. Still the best general survey of the subject, in my view, is Nicholas J. Wheeler (2000), *Saving Strangers: Humanitarian Intervention in International Society*, Oxford: Oxford University Press. From a public policy perspective a very interesting effort to establish the basis for a limited right of humanitarian intervention is provided by The International Commission on Intervention and State Sovereignty (2001), *Responsibility to Protect*, Ottawa: International Development Research Centre.

2. E.g. the participants in Roundtable (2003), 'Evaluating the Pre-emptive Use of Force', *Ethics and International Affairs* 17 (1).
3. Tony Blair (2004), 'PM warns of continuing global terror threat', speech made on 5.3.04. http://www.pm.gov.uk/output/Page5461.asp 28.9.04. In this speech, Blair recalls arguments made in Tony Blair (1999), 'Doctrine of International Community', speech made on 24.4.99. http://www.pm.gov.uk/output/Page1297.asp.
4. Elshtain provides a justification for what she labels 'pre-emption' but which would seem to be closer to preventative war in the ways in which these terms are more generally used. Jean Bethke Elshtain (2004), *Just War Against Terror: The Burden of American Power in a Violent World*, New York: Basic Books, pp. 184–91. For a discussion of the usage of these terms and the distinction between them, see Richard K. Betts (2003), 'Striking First: A History of Thankfully Lost Opportunities', *Ethics and International Affairs* 17 (1). Also Allen Buchanan and Robert O. Keohane (2004), 'Governing the Preventive Use of Force', *Ethics and International Affairs* 18 (1).
5. Stephen M. Walt and John J. Mearsheimer (2003), 'An Unnecessary War', *Foreign Policy* 134 (Jan./Feb.).
6. Although he has distanced himself from this characterisation of the position in more recent work (Chris Brown (2002), *Sovereignty, Rights and Justice: International Political Theory Today*, Cambridge: Polity), amongst the best expositions of the problem in these terms remains Chris Brown (1992), *International Relations Theory: New Normative Approaches*, Brighton: Harvester Wheatsheaf. From a very different perspective Barry Buzan argues that a similar logjam between pluralist and solidarist conceptions in English school theory has also resulted in a debate over human rights and intervention, for example, that is struggling to throw new light on this complex issue. Barry Buzan (2004), *From International to World Society? English School Theory and the Social Structure of Globalisation*, Cambridge: Cambridge University Press, pp. 45–62, 139–60.
7. E.g. Wheeler, *Saving Strangers*, especially Chapter 1. Fernando Téson (1998), *Humanitarian Intervention: An Enquiry into Law and Morality*, Dobbs Ferry: Transnational Publishers. ICISS, *Responsibility to Protect*. For an alternative approach that possesses merit but has not really caught on, see Oliver Ramsbotham (1997), 'Humanitarian Intervention 1990–95: A need to Reconceptualize?' *Review of International Studies* 23 (4).
8. Elshtain provides perhaps the strongest defence of US action in Just War terms, at least in terms of rhetoric if not necessarily in terms of persuasiveness. *Just War Against Terror*, pp. 46–58, 182–91. Also Nicholas J. Wheeler (2002), 'Dying for Enduring Freedom: Accepting Responsibility for Civilian Casualties in the War Against Terrorism', *International Relations* 16 (2); Andrew Hurrell (2002), ' "There are No Rules" (George W. Bush): International Order After September 11', *International Relations* 16 (2).
9. E.g. Barry Buzan (2002), 'Who May We Bomb?' in Ken Booth and Tim Dunne (eds), *Worlds in Collision: Terror and the Future of Global Order*,

Basingstoke: Macmillan. For a very critical response, see Martin Shaw, 'Who May We Bomb: A Reply to Barry Buzan', http://www.theglobal-site.ac.uk/justpeace/111ashaw.htm.

10. Richard Little (2000), 'The English School's Contribution to the Study of International Relations', *European Journal of International Relations* 6 (3).

11. See, for example, Hedley Bull (1977), *The Anarchical Society: A Study of Order in World Politics*, London: Macmillan. Hedley Bull (1984), *Justice in International Relations: The Hagey Lectures*, Ontario: University of Waterloo Press. Barry Buzan, *From International to World Society?* pp. 45–62. Nicholas J. Wheeler (1992), 'Pluralist or Solidarist Conceptions of International Society', *Millennium* 21 (3). Wheeler, *Saving Strangers*, especially Chapter 1.

12. E.g. Wheeler, *Saving Strangers*.

13. The English school, in common with a lot of international relations theory, arguably has a poorly developed and rather implicit theory of the state, a rather surprising situation given the centrality of the state in international relations. Nevertheless, the idea of the state as being understood in broadly liberal terms, even in liberal-contractual terms, does not seem a difficult claim to make on the basis of a representative sample of English school work. A comparatively clear instance comes in Hedley Bull (1979), 'The State's Positive Role in World Affairs', *Dædalus* 108 (4). For a recent analysis of thinking about the state in IR theory, particularly the English school, that makes a similar point about the liberal tenor of much of this work and the need for greater engagement with its normative dimension, see Christian Reus-Smit (1999), *The Moral Purpose of the State: Culture, Social Identity and Institutional Rationality in International Relations*, Princeton, NJ: Princeton University Press.

14. This is an argument that I have, previously, attempted to elaborate and defend. There is therefore an element of self-refutation in this chapter. See John Williams (1999), 'The Ethics of Borders and the Borders of Ethics: International Society and Rights and Duties of Special Beneficence', *Global Society* 13 (4).

15. The clearest example of this effort to introduce rigour is Buzan, *From International to World Society?* but work by Joao Almeida, Tim Dunne, Andrew Hurrell, Richard Little, Hidemi Suganami, Nick Wheeler and others has also made important contributions to exploring and clarifying the methodology, concepts and normative dimensions of English school theory.

16. E.g. Hedley Bull was able to confidently assert that 'The starting point of international relations is the existence of *states*...each of which possesses and asserts sovereignty in relation to a portion of the earth's surface and a particular segment of the human population.' Bull, *Anarchical Society*, p. 10 emphasis in original.

17. Bull, *Anarchical Society*, although it is worth noting that Bull claims that this book is *not* a defence of the existing international society, his scepticism about alternative ordering arrangements generating viable bases for the provision of order and his generally problematic attempts to resist

ascribing order prior status in comparison with other goals, such as peace or justice, lead me to see the book as a defence of the Westphalian system. See John Williams (2006), 'Order and Society', in Richard Little and John Williams (eds), *The Anarchical Society in a Globalized World*, Basingstoke: Palgrave. Also, Robert H. Jackson (2000), *The Global Covenant: Human Conduct in a World of States*, Oxford: Oxford University Press. James Mayall (1990), *Nationalism and International Society*, Cambridge: Cambridge University Press. James Mayall (2000), *World Politics: Progress and Its Limits*, Cambridge: Polity.

18. The origins of this taxonomy are generally seen as lying in the work of Martin Wight, see Martin Wight (1991), *International Theory: The Three Traditions*, edited by Brian Porter and Gabriele Wight, Leicester: Leicester University Press.

19. Bull, *Anarchical Society*, p. 10.

20. Bull, *Anarchical Society*, p. 5.

21. Edward Keene (2002), *Beyond the Anarchical Society: Grotius, Colonialism and Order in World Politics*, Cambridge: Cambridge University Press.

22. Andrew Hurrell (2003), 'International Law and the Making and Unmaking of Boundaries', in Allen Buchanan and Margaret Moore (eds), *States, Nations and Borders: The Ethics of Making Boundaries*, Cambridge: Cambridge University Press.

23. Brown, *Sovereignty, Rights and Justice*, p. 46.

24. Buzan, *From International to World Society?* especially pp. 90–160. Buzan's reformulation almost completely replaces Wight's notion of three traditions and the resultant taxonomic schema with which the English school has rubbed along, arguably since the 1950s. In terms of its clarity of vision, analytical rigour and careful theoretical construction it is unsurpassed and of great value to English school theorists, even those who are likely to find the focus on the structural level of analysis and the heavy reliance on a Wendtian mode of social constructivism unsatisfactory.

25. John Williams (2005), 'Pluralism, Solidarism and the Emergence of World Society in English School Theory', *International Relations* 19 (1).

26. The poverty of the conception of world society in traditional English school theory is one of Buzan's key, and most telling, points. Buzan, *From International to World Society?* pp. 26–62.

27. Little, 'The English School's Contribution'.

28. Timothy Dunne (1995), 'The Social Construction of International Society', *European Journal of International Relations* 1 (3).

29. The idea of a 'classical method', as defended by Bull in the 1960s, has received an important contemporary re-statement in Jackson, *Global Covenant*, pp. 44–96. See also Hedley Bull (1969), 'International Theory: The Case for the Classical Approach', in Klaus Knorr and James N. Rosenau (eds), *Contending Approaches to International Relations*, Princeton: Princeton University Press. For a rather different take on a 'classical approach', see Richard Shapcott (2004), 'IR as Practical Philosophy: Defining a "Classical Approach"', *British Journal of Politics and International Relations* 6 (3).

30. Alexander Wendt (1999), *Social Theory of International Politics*, Cambridge: Cambridge University Press.
31. E.g. (2000), 'Forum on Wendt', *Review of International Studies* 26 (1).
32. This reaches its height, as far as authors who can reasonably be regarded as drawing on or developing the English school tradition is concerned, in the work of Andrew Linklater. See in particular Andrew Linklater (1998), *The Transformation of Political Community: Ethical Foundations for a Post-Westphalian Era*, Cambridge: Polity.
33. Wendt, *Social Theory*, only considers the possibility of different 'cultures' of what we can reasonably see as international societies, that is societies of states. There is, therefore, a good deal of work to be done to include politically significant actors that are not states and that do not necessarily operate within a conception of international politics that is state-based. Buzan represents the most concerted effort to utilise Wendt's work as a methodological basis for a re-formulated English school, but he, too, notes the problems that this brings and the need to add considerably to Wendt's approach. Buzan, *From International to World Society?*
34. The literature on sovereignty has grown sharply in recent years, much of it critical of the sort of position sketched here, although almost all seems to accept that whilst the historical accuracy or reality in practice of this account is doubtful, its rhetorical power and position as assumed standard to be attained remain. For one of the best-known critiques, see Stephen D. Krasner (1999), *Sovereignty – Organized Hypocrisy*, Princeton: Princeton University Press. A useful summary of much recent literature can be found in David A. Lake (2003), 'The New Sovereignty in International Relations', *International Studies Review* 5 (3).
35. A classic statement of this position, still very widely quoted, comes from R. J. Vincent (1974), *Non-Intervention and International Order*, Princeton: Princeton University Press.
36. E.g. Brown, *Sovereignty, Rights and Justice*, pp. 79–80, 97–8.
37. This is a précis of the description offered by a number of English school writers, especially those more closely associated with the pluralist wing of the school, including Hedley Bull, Robert Jackson, James Mayall and Alan James.
38. This kind of account could be drawn from almost any textbook in international relations, although it should be noted that such a straightforward telling of the story has come under growing fire, see Krasner, *Sovereignty – Organized Hypocrisy*; Benno Teschke (2003), *The Myth of 1648: Class, Geopolitics and the Making of Modern International Relations*, London: Verso.
39. E.g. Hedley Bull and Adam Watson (eds) (1984), *The Expansion of International Society*, Oxford: Clarendon. Adam Watson (1992), *The Evolution of International Society*, London: Routledge.
40. Brown, *Sovereignty, Rights and Justice*, pp. 188, 192–200.
41. It is striking, for example, that in discussions of the war on terror and the need for the use of force against Iraq in 2003, senior British government ministers felt the need to refer to the Peace of Westphalia, stressing how,

in their view, things had changed since 2001. Jack Straw (2004) 'We must engage in Europe and in the wider world', speech delivered 21 April, http://www.fco.gov.uk/servlet/Front?pagename = OpenMarket/Xcelerate/ ShowPage&c = Page&cid = 1007029391647&a = KArticle&aid = 107998000 4115.

42. Adam Watson argues that a system that formally claims sovereign equality for all its members is unusual in relation to the whole history of international systems, where some formal recognition of the special status of leading members via ideas such as hegemony and suzerainty are far more common than either the anarchy of Westphalia or its polar opposite, empire. This causes Watson to propose a 'pendulum' theory, whereby 'swings' of the pendulum towards either anarchy or empire are likely to be difficult to maintain, with the pendulum preferring to come to rest somewhere around the 'hegemony' position. Watson, *Evolution of International Society*.

43. Bull, *Anarchical Society*, pp. 38–40.

44. Bull, *Anarchical Society*, pp. 24–38. For a helpful summary of the debate over the status of non-European peoples, particularly in Latin America, and its relationship to some more contemporary discussions of human rights, see Chris Brown (2000), 'Cultural Diversity and International Political Theory: From the *Requirement* to "Mutual Respect"?' *Review of International Studies* 26 (2). For an analysis of the role of the native peoples of Latin America in the creation of the idea of a 'state of nature' in European political thought, and the influence this had on international relations, see Beate Jahn (2000), *The Cultural Construction of International Relations: The Invention of the State of Nature*, Basingstoke: Palgrave.

45. James Mayall, for example, a leading pluralist figure, argues that international law is 'the bedrock institution on which the idea of international society stands or falls'. Mayall, *World Politics*, p. 94. Bull makes a similar point: 'The first function of international law has been to identify, as the supreme normative principle of the political organisation of mankind, the idea of a society of sovereign states. This is … the fundamental or constitutional principle of world politics in the present era. Order in the great society of all mankind has been attained, during the present phase of the modern states system, through general acceptance of the principle that men [*sic*] and territory are divided into states, each with its proper sphere of authority, but linked together by a common set of rules.' *Anarchical Society*, p. 140.

46. Bull veers towards the latter, e.g. Bull, *Anarchical Society*, pp. 276, 293–5, although he recognises there is normative force in arguments for a more cosmopolitan version of international society. Bull, *Justice in International Relations*, p. 12. Jackson tends to take a more power-oriented line, regarding assertions of ethical universalism on the basis of Western ideas like human rights as hubris. Jackson, *Global Covenant*, pp. 366–70.

47. John Rawls (1999), *A Theory of Justice*, Oxford: Oxford University Press; John Rawls (1993), *Political Liberalism*, New York: Columbia University Press; Brian Barry (1995), *Justice as Impartiality*, Oxford: Clarendon; Henry Shue (1996), *Basic Rights: Subsistence, Affluence and US Foreign Policy (Second edition)*, Princeton: Princeton University Press.
48. Andrew Linklater (1990), *Beyond Realism and Marxism: Critical Theory in International Relations*, Basingstoke: Macmillan; Linklater, *Transformation of Political Community*.
49. Richard Shapcott (2001), *Justice, Community and Dialogue in International Relations*, Cambridge: Cambridge University Press.
50. Nigel Dower (1998), *World Ethics: The New Agenda*, Edinburgh: Edinburgh University Press.
51. Peter Jones (2001), 'Human Rights and Diverse Cultures: Continuity or Discontinuity' in Simon Caney and Peter Jones (eds), *Human Rights and Global Diversity*, London: Frank Cass.
52. Tim Dunne and Nicholas J. Wheeler (1996), 'Hedley Bull's Pluralism of the Intellect and Solidarism of the Will', *International Affairs* 72 (1).
53. See the different analyses of the nature, role and effectiveness of human rights in international relations in Tim Dunne and Nicholas J. Wheeler (eds) (1999), *Human Rights in Global Politics*, Cambridge: Cambridge University Press.
54. Barbara F. Walter (2003), 'Explaining the intractability of territorial conflict', *International Studies Review* 5 (4).
55. On the idea of 'global prohibition regimes', see Ethan A. Nadelman (1990), 'Global Prohibition Regimes: The Evolution of Norms in International Society', *International Organization* 44 (4).
56. One of the strongest examples of this sort of claim, which is quite widespread in the literature on cosmopolitan ethics in international political theory, is the 'cosmopolitan democracy' project particularly associated with the work of David Held and Daniele Archibugi. E.g. David Held (1995), *Democracy and the Global Order: From the Modern State to Cosmopolitan Governance*, Cambridge: Polity.
57. Nicholas J. Wheeler (1996), 'Guardian Angel or Global Gangster: A Review of the Ethical Claims of International Society', *Political Studies* 44 (1).
58. For an analysis that emphasises this as being the logic of Bull's position in particular, although it could be applied to other pluralists like Jackson, Mayall and James, too, without fundamental alteration, see Williams, 'Order and Society'.
59. Jackson, *Global Covenant*, pp. 332–3.
60. See his discussion of Enlightenment and post-Enlightenment thought, for example. Brown, *Sovereignty, Rights and Justice*, pp. 38–56.
61. Thus almost all writers on 'global governance' reject the idea of world government. This particular rejection, on ethical grounds, can be traced back at least to Kant, who's scheme for perpetual peace involved no more than a confederation of states. Immanuel Kant (1970 [1795]), *Perpetual*

Peace, in H. Reiss (ed.), *Kant's Political Writings*, Cambridge: Cambridge University Press.

62. Held, *Democracy and the Global Order*, pp. 66–8, 241–2.
63. E.g. Robin Atfield (2002), 'Global Citizenship and the Global Environment', in Nigel Dower and John Williams (eds), *Global Citizenship: A Critical Reader*, Edinburgh: Edinburgh University Press.
64. E.g. Held, *Democracy and the Global Order*, pp. 127–8.
65. Held, *Democracy and the Global Order*, pp. 219–86.
66. There is an interesting instance of this kind of logic in relation to one of the most important institutional innovations in international relations of recent years, the ICC. The ICC is only able to take on responsibility for the trial of those suspected of war crimes or crimes against humanity covered by its statute once it is clear that the appropriate national authority is unwilling or unable to pursue effective and proper legal procedures. Jason Ralph (2005), 'International Society, the International Criminal Court and American Foreign Policy', *Review of International Studies* 31 (1).
67. For an account and analysis of the practice of returning terrorism subjects to states where torture is used, see Human Rights Watch (2005), *Still at Risk: Diplomatic Assurances No Safeguard Against Torture*, New York: Human Rights Watch, available at http://hrw.org/reports/2005/eca0405/. Also Human Rights Watch (2004), *The United States' 'Disappeared': The CIA's Long-Term 'Ghost Detainees'*, New York, Human Rights Watch, available at http://hrw.org/backgrounder/usa/us1004/index.htm which alleges the use of torture by CIA agents on non-US citizens held *in communicado* outside the United States, in countries such as Saudi Arabia, Yemen and Algeria.
68. This kind of argument draws on an ethic of statesmanship that is often associated with classical realism, although this is not in any way to claim that realists defend torture. See Joel H. Rosenthal (1991), *Righteous Realists: Political Realism, Responsible Power and American Culture in the Nuclear Age*, Baton Rouge: Louisiana State University Press; Jonathan Haslam (2002), *No Virtue Like Necessity: Realist Thought in International Relations Since Machiavelli*, New Have CT: Yale University Press.
69. Perhaps the most famous recent defence of the use of torture is Alan M. Dershowitz (2002), 'The Case for Torture Warrants', http://www.law.harvard.edu/faculty/dershowitz/Articles/torturewarrants.html. However, Dershowitz does not discriminate between citizens and non-citizens in his paper. Arguments put forward by some members of the George W. Bush Administration that the legal prohibition against torture does not apply to non-US citizens interrogated abroad does point towards such a position, though.
70. This is also the position in international law, argue most human rights groups. E.g. Human Rights Watch, *Still at Risk*, pp. 7–17. Interestingly, Dershowitz also notes this to be the legal position, 'The Case for Torture Warrants'.

71. Ken Booth (1995), 'Human Wrongs and International Relations', *International Affairs* 71 (1).
72. E.g. Martha Nussbaum (1996), 'Cosmopolitanism and Patriotism', in Joshua Cohen (ed.), *For Love of Country: Debating the Limits of Patriotism*, Boston: Beacon Books.
73. This appeals to a classic liberal exposition of the idea of citizenship associated with T. H. Marshall (1973), *Class, Citizenship and Social Development*, Westport CN: Greenwood Press.
74. Williams, 'The Ethics of Borders'.
75. Peter Singer (1985 [1972]), 'Famine, Affluence and Morality', in Charles R. Beitz *et al.* (eds), *International Ethics*, Princeton: Princeton University Press.
76. A helpful summary of these arguments on this point can be found in Brown, *Sovereignty, Rights and Justice*, pp. 179–86.
77. A variety of defences of patriotism against a cosmopolitan ethical perspective can be found in the responses to Martha Nussbaum's famous piece 'Cosmopolitanism and Patriotism'. Cohen (ed.), *For Love of Country*. Also Michael Walzer (1983), *Spheres of Justice*, New York: Basic Books.
78. E.g. Mayall, *Nationalism and International Society*.
79. E.g. Richard Falk (2000), 'An Emergent Matrix of Citizenship: Complex, Uneven and Fluid', in Dower and Williams (eds), *Global Citizenship*.
80. The author was fortunate enough in January 2005 to enjoy a tour of parts of the old city given by the former deputy mayor of Jerusalem, and noted commentator on political geography in Israel–Palestine, Meron Benvenisti, who pointed out many of the complex border issues affecting the city. See also, Menachem Klein (2005), 'New and Old Walls in Jerusalem', *Political Geography* 24 (1).
81. Leaving aside the issue of the land lying within the width of the line, where the line was drawn with a thick pen on an inappropriately scaled map, as was the case with the 'green line' dividing post-1967 Israel from the 'Occupied Territories'.
82. Frances Harbour argues that the idea of rights and duties of special beneficence has great utility because it is one of very few ethical ideas that can be found in all known human societies. Frances V. Harbour (1995), 'Basic Moral Values: A Shared Core', *Ethics and International Affairs* 9.
83. E.g. Jonathan Eyal (1993), *Europe and Yugoslavia: Lessons From a Failure*, London: Royal United Services Institute.
84. John Kampfner (2003), *Blair's Wars*, London: Free Press, pp. 65–77.
85. E.g. Bruce D. Jones (1995), 'Intervention Without Borders: Humanitarian Intervention in Rwanda', *Millennium* 24 (2). For a damning verdict on the actions of all members of the international community, see Linda Melvern (2000), *Rwanda – a Nation Betrayed*, London: Zed Press.
86. President George W. Bush, or perhaps more accurately his speechwriter, appears to be almost unable to compose an address on US foreign policy that does not include the phrase 'freedom-loving peoples'. Listing specific instances is therefore probably unnecessary.

87. George W. Bush (2001), 'Address to a Joint Session of Congress and the American People', available at http://www.whitehouse.gov/news/releases/2001/09/20010920-8.html.
88. Bull, *Anarchical Society*; Jackson, *Global Covenant*.
89. This is the kind of solidarist, confederative interstate society that Buzan describes as a part of his diagrammatic reformulation of English school theory. Buzan, *From International to World Society?* p. 159.
90. It is worth stressing that Buzan is critical of this assumption, seeing it as far from automatic, and analytically damaging. He emphasises how there is no requirement for what he labels 'convergence' in an interstate society to take place on the basis of liberal values, or necessarily as a result of a deeply held common belief, with coercion potentially playing a dominant role. Buzan, *From International to World Society?* p. 160.
91. Buzan, *From International to World Society?* especially pp. 6–62, 90–160.
92. Buzan, *From International to World Society?*, pp. 139–60.
93. Dale C. Copeland (2003), 'A Realist Critique of the English School', *Review of International Studies* 29 (3).
94. Blair, 'PM warns of continuing global terror threat', Straw 'We must engage in Europe and in the wider world'. Jack Straw (2002), 'Principles of a modern global community', speech delivered on 10.4.02. http://www.fco.gov.uk/servlet/Front?pagename = OpenMarket/Xcelerate/ShowPage &c=Page&cid=1007029391647&a=KArticle&aid=1018466002161. Jack Straw (2002), 'Failed and failing states', speech delivered on 6.9.02. http://www.fco.gov.uk/servlet/Front?pagename=OpenMarket/Xcelerate/ShowPage &c=Page&cid= 1007029391647&a=KArticle&aid=1031273860289.
95. Kant, *Perpetual Peace*.
96. John Agnew and Stuart Corbridge (1995), *Mastering Space: Hegemony, Territory and Political Economy*, London: Routledge.
97. For a summary of environmental theory in international relations, see Matthew Paterson (2005), 'Green Politics', in Scott Burchill *et al.*, *International Relations Theory (Third edition)*, Basingstoke: Palgrave.
98. A good summary of the entrenchment of the territorial integrity rule is provided by Mark W. Zacher (2002), 'The Territorial Integrity Norm: International Boundaries and the Use of Force', *International Organization* 55 (2).

4   Valuing borders (and bordering values?)

1. For some exceptions, see, in chronological order, Paul Saurette (1996), ' "I Mistrust all Systematizers and Avoid Them": Nietzsche, Arendt and the Crisis of the Will to Order in International Relations Theory', *Millennium* 25 (1); Anthony F. Lang, Jr (2002), *Agency and Ethics: The Politics of Military Intervention*, Albany, NY: SUNY Press; John Williams (2002), 'Toleration, Territorial Borders and the English School', *Review of International Studies* 28 (4); Douglas Klusmeyer and Astri Suhrke (2002), 'Comprehending "Evil": Challenges for Law and Policy', *Ethics and*

International Affairs 16 (1); Patricia Owens (2003), 'Accidents Don't Just Happen: The Liberal Politics of High-Tech "Humanitarian" War', *Millennium* 32 (4); Anthony F. Lang, Jr and John Williams (eds) (2005), *Hannah Arendt and International Relations: Readings Across the Lines*, New York: Palgrave.

2. E.g. Susan Mendus (1989), *Toleration and the Limits of Liberalism*, Basingstoke: Macmillan.

3. Glenn Tinder (1976), *Tolerance: Toward a New Civility*, Amherst, MA: University of Massachusetts Press, p. 8.

4. Mendus, *Toleration and the Limits of Liberalism*, pp. 8–18.

5. Robert H. Jackson (2000), *The Global Covenant: Human Conduct in a World of States*, Oxford: Oxford University Press, p. 139.

6. E.g. Richard Bellamy (1999), *Liberalism and Pluralism: Towards a Politics of Compromise*, London: Routledge, pp. 46–9.

7. This is not just a view on the more extreme right, but has been expressed by figures such as former French President and Chairman of the convention that produced the EU's ill-fated constitutional treaty, Valery Giscard d'Estaing. See http://news.bbc.co.uk/1/hi/world/europe/2420697.stm.

8. E.g. Steve Bruce (2003), 'Religion', in Robert Singh (ed.), *Governing America: The Politics of a Divided Democracy*, Oxford: Oxford University Press.

9. E.g. Cynthia Enloe (1989), *Bananas, Beaches and Bases: Making Feminist Sense of International Politics*, London: Pandora Press, pp. 1–18, 195–201.

10. John Horton and Susan Mendus (eds) (1991), *John Locke 'A Letter Concerning Toleration' in Focus*, London: Routledge, pp. 36–7.

11. Selina Chen (1998), 'Locke's Political Arguments for Toleration', *History of Political Thought* 19 (2): 169.

12. Robin Cook (1997), 'Human Rights into a New Century', speech delivered on 17.7.97. http://www.fco.gov.uk/servlet/Front?pagename=Open Market/Xcelerate/ShowPage&c=Page&cid=1007029391647&a=KArticle&aid=1013 618392902. For a critique of the consequences of such a claim, see Chris Brown, 'Cultural Diversity and International Political Theory: From the *Requirement* to "Mutual Respect"?' *Review of International Studies* 26 (2), 2000, pp. 199–213.

13. Hedley Bull (1977), *The Anarchical Society: A Study of Order in World Politics*, London: Macmillan, p. 16.

14. John Williams (1999), 'The Ethical Basis of Humanitarian Intervention, the Security Council and Yugoslavia', *International Peacekeeping* 6 (2).

15. On Kosovo, see Nicholas J. Wheeler (2001), 'Humanitarian Vigilantes or Legal Entrepreneurs: Enforcing Human Rights in International Society', in Simon Caney and Peter Jones (eds), *Human Rights and Global Diversity* (Ilford: Frank Cass). The UK Attorney General, Lord Goldsmith, picks out the Kosovo 'precedent' in his discussion of possible legal bases for British military action against Iraq in March 2003. Lord Goldsmith, 'Iraq: Resolution 1441', available at http://www.number-10.gov.uk/output/Page7445.asp.

16. Williams, 'The Ethical Basis of Humanitarian Intervention, the Security Council and Yugoslavia', p. 18.
17. Nicholas J. Wheeler (2000), *Saving Strangers: Humanitarian Intervention in International Society*, Oxford: Oxford University Press, especially Chapter 1. Michael Walzer (2002), *Just and Unjust Wars: A Moral Argument with Historical Illustrations (Third edition)*, New York: Basic Books, pp. 101–108.
18. Walzer, *Just and Unjust Wars*, p. 107.
19. Michael Walzer (1994), *Thick and Thin: Moral Argument at Home and Abroad*, London: University of Notre Dame Press.
20. Chris Brown (2002), *Sovereignty, Rights and Jutsice: International Political Theory Today*, Cambridge: Polity, pp. 88–95, especially 90–1.
21. Thus we are now following Buzan's notion of world society, which excludes states. Barry Buzan (2004), *From International to World Society? English School Theory and the Social Structure of Globalisation*, Cambridge: Cambridge University Press, pp. 90–138.
22. This is something to which a range of Walzer's work contributes, but is most clearly set out in Michael Walzer (1983), *Spheres of Justice: A Defence of Pluralism and Equality*, Oxford: Robertson.
23. Chen, 'Locke's Political Arguments for Toleration' offers a more positive assessment than this but, in my view, this rests on cosmopolitan assumptions about universal rationality that open this assessment to similar charges that we will apply to Mill, below.
24. E.g. Jackson, *Global Covenant*, pp. 21.
25. Both Bull and Jackson highlight prudence as a political virtue. Hedley Bull (1984), *Justice in International Relations: The Hagey Lectures*, Waterloo, Ontario: University of Waterloo Press. Jackson, *Global Covenant*, pp. 51–8.
26. Bull, *Anarchical Society*, pp. 134–5.
27. The best summary of Just War thinking, and probably the best defence of its utility, remains Walzer, *Just and Unjust Wars*. Most of the points in the next paragraph can be found there.
28. For example, Barry Buzan does not include Inter-Governmental Organisations (IGOs), like the UN, in his account of 'world society' on the grounds that they lack significant enough 'actorly' qualities to differentiate them from states. He instead sees them as contributing to the interaction capacity of international society.
29. Elshtain, *Just War Against Terror*, pp. 85–98.
30. This summary borrows from Mendus, *Toleration and the Limits of Liberalism*, pp. 22–68.
31. Bull, *Justice in International Relations*, especially the second lecture on 'The Coming Revolt Against the West'.
32. Bull, *Anarchical Society*, p. 317.
33. David L. Blaney and Naeem Inayatullah (2000), 'The Westphalian Deferral', *International Studies Review* 2 (2).
34. The label is borrowed from Susan Strange (1999), 'The Westfailure System', *Review of International Studies* 25 (3).

35. Elshtain, *Just War Against Terror*.
36. John Williams (2005), 'Hannah Arendt and the International Space In-Between?' in Lang and Williams (eds), *Hannah Arendt and International Relations*, p. 206.
37. Douglas Klusmeyer (2005), 'Hannah Arendt's Critical *Realism*: Power, Justice and Responsibility', in Lang and Williams (eds), *Hannah Arendt and International Relations*.
38. Klusmeyer and Suhrke, 'Comprehending Evil'.
39. Hannah Arendt (1958), *The Human Condition*, Chicago: University of Chicago Press, p. 8.
40. Arendt, *Human Condition*, pp. 181–2.
41. The best English school account of nationalism remains James Mayall (1990), *Nationalism and International Society*, Cambridge: Cambridge University Press. The idea of 'ethno-nationalism' can be found summarised in Anthony D. Smith (1991), *National Identity*, London: Penguin.
42. Arendt, *Human Condition*, pp. 175–6.
43. Arendt, *Human Condition*, pp. 175–207.
44. Arendt, *Human Condition*, pp. 181–92.
45. E.g. Hannah Arendt (1973), *Origins of Totalitarianism (New edition with Added Prefaces)*, New York: Harcourt Brace Jovanovich, p. 477.
46. Hannah Arendt (1977), 'The Concept of History', in Hannah Arendt, *Between Past and Future*, New York: Penguin Books.
47. E.g. Arendt, *Human Condition*, pp. 7–21, 175–247.
48. Samuel P. Huntington (1996), *The Clash of Civilizations and the Remaking of World Order*, New York: Simon and Schuster.
49. Arendt, *Origins of Totalitarianism*; Hannah Arendt (1963), *Eichmann in Jerusalem: A Report on the Banality of Evil*, London: Faber and Faber.
50. Hannah Arendt (1970), 'On Humanity in Dark Times: Thoughts About Lessing', in *Men in Dark Times*, London: Jonathan Cape, p. 18.
51. This is a key argument made by Klusmeyer in his analysis of the failure of Morgenthau and Kennan to fully appreciate the political significance of the Holocaust. Klusmeyer, 'Hannah Arendt's Critical *Realism*'.
52. A good discussion of Arendt's arguments on human rights is available in Bridget Cotter (2005), Hannah Arendt and the Right to Have Rights', in Lang and Williams (eds), *Hannah Arendt and International Relations*. See also Arendt, *Origins of Totalitarianism*, pp. 279–302.
53. Arendt, *Eichmann in Jerusalem*, p. 247.
54. Arendt, *Origins of Totalitarianism*, p. 477.
55. Margaret Canovan (1974), *The Political Thought of Hannah Arendt*, London: J. M. Dent, pp. 57–65.
56. Hannah Arendt (1963), *On Revolution*, London: Faber and Faber.
57. Arendt, *Origins of Totalitarianism*, pp. 290–302.
58. John Williams with Anthony F. Lang, Jr (2005), 'Introduction', in Lang and Williams (eds), *Hannah Arendt and International Relations*, pp. 3–9. See also Bhikhu Parekh (1981), *Hannah Arendt and the Search for a New Political Philosophy*, London: Macmillan; Philip Hansen (1993), *Hannah Arendt: Politics, History and Citizenship*, Cambridge: Polity; Margaret Canovan

(1992), *Hannah Arendt: A Reinterpretation of her Political Thought*, Cambridge: Cambridge University Press.

59. This comes through most clearly in Arendt, *On Revolution*.

60. Arendt, *Human Condition*, p. 245.

61. Margaret Canovan (1988), 'Friendship, Truth and Politics: Hannah Arendt and Toleration', in Susan Mendus (ed.), *Justifying Toleration*, Cambridge: Cambridge University Press.

62. Arendt, 'On Humanity in Dark Times', p. 4.

63. Arendt, 'On Humanity in Dark Times', p. 4.

64. Jackson argues that '...there are fewer than 20,000 people worldwide who are the primary subjects of international ethics', and of these probably only 1000 really matter. Jackson, *Global Covenant*, p. 134.

65. Williams, 'Hannah Arendt and the International In-Between?'

66. Hansen, *Hannah Arendt: Politics, History and Citizenship*, pp. 89–128.

67. Margaret Canovan (1996), 'Hannah Arendt as a Conservative Thinker', in Larry May and Jerome Kohn (eds), *Hannah Arendt: Twenty Years Later*, Cambridge, MA: MIT Press, pp. 14–21.

68. Arendt, *Origins of Totalitarianism*, pp. 389, 391.

69. E.g. Arendt, *Human Condition*, p. 26; Hannah Arendt (1972), 'On Violence' in Hannah Arendt, *Crises of the Republic*, New York: Harcourt Brace Jovanovich.

70. E.g. Peter Andreas (2003), 'Redrawing the Line: Borders and Security in the Twenty-first century', *International Security* 28 (2).

71. Canovan, 'Friendship, Truth and Politics', pp. 196–7.

72. Patricia Owens notes how at times Arendt can appear to use the idea of violence as a way to deny 'political' status to things she disapproved of Patricia Owens (2005), 'Hannah Arendt, Violence and the Inescapable Fact of Humanity', in Lang and Williams (eds), *Hannah Arendt and International Relations*, pp. 50–51.

73. Colin S. Gray, 'The future is the Past – With GPS', *Review of International Studies* 25 (Special issue).

74. James Bohman (1996), 'The Moral Costs of Political Pluralism: The Dilemmas of Difference and Equality in Arendt's "Reflections on Little Rock"', in May and Kohn (eds), *Hannah Arendt: Twenty Years Later*, p. 60.

75. Arendt, *Eichmann in Jerusalem*, pp. 255–6.

76. In a striking instance of this desire to preserve the 'apolitical' nature of the idea of humanitarianism, a number of INGOs object to the use of the term 'humanitarian intervention' because of the deeply political nature of intervention being seen to sully humanitarianism. The International Commission on Intervention and State Sovereignty (ICISS), in its report, *Responsibility to Protect*, coined the phrase 'intervention for human protection purposes' to assuage these concerns. However, there seems no sign yet that this terminology will catch on. ICISS (2001), *Responsibility to Protect*, Ottowa: International Development Research Centre, p. 9.

77. Arendt, *Origins of Totalitarianism*, p. ix.
78. The literature on both is extensive, but this conclusion would appear to receive general support, including from those who played a role in both. See Mohammed Sahnoun, 'Mixed Intervention in Somalia and the Great Lakes: Culture, Neutrality and the Military', and Romeo Dallaire, 'The End of Innocence: Rwanda 1994', both in Jonathan More (ed.) (1998), *Hard Choices: Moral Dilemmas in Humanitarian Intervention*, Oxford: Rowman and Littlefield.
79. Although Elshtain appears to offer something close to this. Elshtain, *Just War Against Terror*, pp. 26–45, 150–60.
80. E.g. Tony Blair (2005), 'Statement on the London Bombings', statement to Parliament delivered on 11.7.05. http://www.pm.gov.uk/output/Page7903.asp, Tony Blair (2005), 'Statement to Monthly Downing Street Press Conference, August 2005', http://www.pm.gov.uk/output/Page8041.asp.
81. Elshatin, *Just War Against Terror*, pp. 14, 71–84.
82. Buzan, *From International to World Society?* pp. 77–87.
83. Andrew Linklater (1998), *The Transformation of Political Community: Ethical Foundations for a Post-Westphalian Era*, Cambridge: Polity. Richard Shapcott (2001), *Justice, Community and Dialogue in International Relations*, Cambridge: Cambridge University Press.

5 Shifting lines in the sand

1. Peter Andreas (2003), 'Redrawing the Line: Borders and Security in the Twenty-first Century', *International Security* 28 (2).
2. E.g. David Newman notes the durability of the territorial border, and the border dispute, and its likely persistence into the future. David Newman (2004), 'Conflict at the Interface: The Impact of Boundaries and Borders on Contemporary Ethno-National Conflict', in Colin Flint (ed.), *The Geography of War and Peace*, Oxford: Oxford University Press.
3. For a survey of this literature, see Klaus Dodds (2001), 'Political Geography III: Critical Geopolitics After Ten Years', *Progress in Human Geography* 25 (3).
4. E.g. Newman, 'Conflict at the Interface'; Thomas Diez (ed.) (2002), *The European Union and the Cyprus Conflict*, Manchester: Manchester University Press; Sumantra Bose (2003), *Kashmir: Roots of Conflict, Paths to Peace*, Cambridge, MA: Harvard University Press.
5. This, it seems to me, is the promise made by crtitical theory's normative project. See Andrew Linklater (1998), *The Transformation of Political Community: Ethical Foundations for a Post-Westphalian Era*, Cambridge: Polity. For a critique, which sees this kind of critical theory as thinly disguised liberalism and lacking the analytical edge that it ought to have

acquired from its Frankfurt School origins, see Beate Jahn (1998), 'Two Steps Forward One Step Back: Critical Theory as the Latest Manifestation of Liberal Internationalism', *Millennium* 27 (3).

6. John Williams (2005), 'Hannah Arendt and an International In-Between?' in Anthony F. Lang, Jr and John Williams (eds), *Hannah Arendt and International Relations: Readings Across the Lines*, New York: Palgrave.

7. Barry Buzan (2004), *From International to World Society? English School Theory and the Social Structure of Globalisation*, Cambridge: Cambridge University Press, pp. 77–87.

8. This is something Buzan stresses in relation to the understanding of the 'depth' of social forms, and which he takes from Wendt. Buzan, *From International to World Society?* pp. 102–8.

9. Mark W. Zacher (2002), 'The Territorial Integrity Norm: International Boundaries and the Use of Force', *International Organization* 55 (2).

10. 'We are living at a time when existing international boundaries are vested with exceptional and, indeed, almost absolute value', Robert H. Jackson (2000), *The Global Covenant: Human Conduct in a World of States*, Oxford: Oxford University Press, p. 327.

11. For a classis account of the way in which national self-determination, for instance, was rendered compatible with the idea of sovereignty and protective of established territorial borders, see Martin Wight (1977), *Systems of States*, Leicester: Leicester University Press, Chapter 6.

12. Susan Strange (1999), 'The Westfailure System', *Review of International Studies*, 25 (3).

13. E.g. F. H. Hinsley (1963), *Power and the Pursuit of Peace: Theory and Practice in the History of Relations Between States*, Cambridge: Cambridge University Press, pp. 33–45.

14. The obvious target here is neo-realism, with its classic statement coming in Kenneth N. Waltz (1979), *Theory of International Politics*, New York: Addison Wesley Longman.

15. The best known statement of this claim is Wendt's. Alexander Wendt (1999), *Social Theory of International Politics*, Cambridge: Cambridge University Press.

16. Although unsustainable to argue that this is the case in all versions, the critical geo-politics literature probably comes closest to this position. For a useful summary, see Dodds, 'Political Geography'. Also important in this sort of portrayal is the kind of radical security studies best represented by Eric Herring. More popularly, the work of John Pilger and Noam Chomsky can also be seen in this light.

17. Nicholas Greenwood Onuf (1990), *World of Our Making: Rules and Rule in Social Theory and International Relations*, Columbia: University of South Carolina Press; Friedrich Kratochwil (1989), *Rules, Norms and Decisions: On the Conditions of Practical and Legal Reasoning in International*

Relations and Domestic Affairs, Cambridge: Cambridge University Press; Wendt, *Social Theory of International Politics*.

18. Linklater, *Transformation of Political Community*.
19. E.g. Mary Kaldor (2003), *Global Civil Society: An Answer to War*, Cambridge: Polity.
20. Thucydides, of course. Thucydides (1923), *History of the Peloponnesian War*, trans. C. F. Smith, London: Loeb Classic Library, p. 98.
21. Buzan, *From International to World Society?*.
22. Buzan, *From International to World Society?* pp. 90–139.
23. John Williams (2005), 'Pluralism, Solidarism and the Emergence of World Society in English School Theory', *International Relations* 19 (1).
24. Williams, 'Pluralism, Solidarism'.
25. Buzan, *From International to World Society?* pp. 39–44, 95–7.
26. The idea of political communities claiming autonomy being 'like units' is a mainstay of neo-realist theory. For a critique of the way in which this effort to close down the influence of the nature of those units misunderstands their unavoidable importance to the nature of the system they form, see John Gerard Ruggie (1998), 'Political Structure and Dynamic Density', in John Gerard Ruggie, *Constructing the World Polity: Essays on Internatonal Institutionalization*, London: Routledge.
27. Bull, *Anarchical Society*, pp. 10, 140
28. Buzan is critical of the failure of much thinking about world society to recognise this weakness and aims to offer a mechanism whereby regionalism can be incorporated into a model of world society, too. *From International to World Society?* pp. 27–44, 205–27.
29. Buzan, *From International to World Society?* pp. 205–27.
30. Amyn B. Sajoo (2004), *Muslim Ethics: Emerging Vistas*, London: I. B. Tauris.
31. I am grateful to Gordon Cheung, and his expertise in the political economy of the Chinese diaspora, for these points.
32. There are a variety of ways of theoretically grounding this kind of argument. For an English school example, see. Jackson, *The Global Covenant*. For a neo-realist line see John J. Mearsheimer (2001), *The Tragedy of Great Power Politics*, New York: W. W. Norton.
33. ICISS (2001), *Responsibility to Protect*, Ottawa: International Development Research Centre.
34. Hannah Arendt (1973), *Origins of Totalitarianism (New edition with added prefaces)*, New York: Harcourt Brace Jovanovich, pp. 389, 391.
35. This, of course, derives from an argument to be found in Kant (1970 [1795]), *Perpetual Peace*, in H. Reiss (ed.), *Kant's Political Writings*, Cambridge: Cambridge University Press.
36. For some recent examples, see Jean Bethke Elshtain (2004), *Just War Against Terror: The Burden of American Power in a Violent World*, New York: Basic Books; Michael Ignatieff (2004), *The Lesser Evil: Political Ethics in an*

Age of Terrorism, Edinburgh: Edinburgh University Press; James Turner Johnson (2001), *Morality and Contemporary Warfare*, New Haven, CT: Yale University Press; Michael Walzer (2004), *Arguing About War*, New Haven, CT: Yale University Press.
37. Malcolm Anderson (1996), *Frontiers: Territory and State Formation in the Modern World*, Cambridge: Polity.

Bibliography

Forum on Wendt. 2000. *Review of International Studies* 26 (1).

How might we live? 2000. *Review of International Studies* 26 (Special issue).

Roundtable: Evaluating the pre-emptive use of force. 2003. *Ethics and International Affairs* 17 (1).

The United States' 'disappeared': the CIA's long-term 'ghost detainees'. 2004. New York: Human Rights Watch [Available from http://hrw.org/backgrounder/usa/us1004/index.htm].

The Prevention of Terrorism Bill: A grave threat to human rights and the rule of law in the UK 2005. London: Amnesty International [Available from http://web.amnesty.org/library/index/engeur450052005].

Still at risk: Diplomatic assurances no safeguard against torture. 2005. New York: Human Rights Watch [Available from http://hrw.org/reports/2005/eca0405/].

Agnew, John and Stuart Corbridge. 1995. *Mastering Space: Hegemony, Territory and Political Economy*. London: Routledge.

Anderson, Malcolm. 1996. *Frontiers: Territory and State Formation in the Modern World*. Cambridge: Polity.

Andreas, Peter. 2003. Redrawing the line: Borders and security in the twenty-first century. *International Security* 28 (2).

Arendt, Hannah. 1958. *The Human Condition*. Chicago: University of Chicago Press.

——. 1963. *Eichmann in Jerusalem: A Report on the Banality of Evil*. London: Faber and Faber.

——. 1963. *On Revolution*. London: Faber and Faber.

——. 1970. On humanity in dark times: Thoughts about Lessing. In *Men in Dark Times*. London: Jonathan Cape.

——. 1972. On violence. In *Crises of the Republic*. New York: Harcourt Brace Jovanovich.

——. 1973. *Origins of Totalitarianism*. New edition with added prefaces, New York: Harcourt Brace Jovanovich.

——. 1977. The concept of history. In *Between Past and Future*. New York: Penguin Books.

Atfield, Robin. 2002. Global citizenship and the global environment. In *Global Citizenship: A Critical Reader*, edited by N. Dower and J. Williams. Edinburgh: Edinburgh University Press.

Barry, Brian. 1995. *Justice as Impartiality*. Oxford: Clarendon.

Beitz, Charles R. 1979. *Political Theory and International Relations*, Princeton, NJ: Princeton University Press.

Bellamy, Richard. 1999. *Liberalism and Pluralism: Towards a Politics of Compromise*. London: Routledge.

Betts, Richard K. 2003. Striking first: A history of thankfully lost opportunities. *Ethics and International Affairs* 17 (1).

Birchfield, Vicki. 2005. Jose Bove and the globalisation countermovement. *Review of International Studies* 31 (3).

Blair, Tony. 1999. *Doctrine of International Community*, speech delivered 24.4.99 [Available from http://www.pm.gov.uk/output/Page1297.asp].

——. 2004. *PM Warns of Continuing Global Terror Threat*, speech delivered 5.3.04 [Available from http://www.pm.gov.uk/output/Page5459.asp].

——. 2005. *Statement on London Bombings*, delivered to Parliament 11.7.05 [Available from http://www.pm.gov.uk/output/Page7903.asp].

——. 2005. *Statement to Monthly Downing Street Press Conference* 5.8.05 [Available from http://www.pm.gov.uk/output/Page8041.asp].

Blake, Gerald. 2001. Borderlands under stress: Some global perspectives. In *Borderlands Under Stress*, edited by M. Pratt and J. A. Brown. London: Kluwer Law International.

Blaney, David L. and Naeem Inayatullah. 2000. The Westphalian deferral. *International Studies Review* 2 (2).

Bohman, James. 1996. The moral costs of political pluralism: The dilemmas of difference and equality in Arendt's 'reflections on Little Rock'. In *Hannah Arendt: Twenty Years Later*, edited by L. May and J. Kohn. Cambrdge, MA: MIT Press.

Booth, Ken. 1995. Human wrongs and international relations. *International Affairs* 71 (1).

Bose, Sumantra. 2003. *Kashmir: Roots of Conflict, Paths to Peace*. Cambridge, MA: Harvard University Press.

Brown, Chris. 1992. *International Relations Theory: New Normative Approaches*. Brighton: Harvester Wheatsheaf.

——. 2000. Cultural diversity and international political theory: From the Requirement to 'mutual respect'. *Review of International Studies* 26 (2).

——. 2001. Cosmopolitanism, world citizenship and global civil society. In *Human Rights and Cultural Diversity*, edited by S. Caney and P. Jones. London: Frank Cass.

——. 2002. *Sovereignty, Rights and Justice: International Political Theory Today*. Cambridge: Polity.

Bruce, Steve. 2003. Religion. In *Governing America: The Politics of a Divided Democracy*, edited by R. Singh. Oxford: Oxford University Press.

Buchanan, Allen and Robert O. Keohane. 2004. Governing the preventive use of force. *Ethics and International Affairs* 18 (1).

Bull, Hedley. 1969. The case for the classical approach. In *Contending Approaches to International Relations*, edited by K. Knorr and J. N. Rosenau. Princeton, NJ: Princeton University Press.

——. 1977. *The Anarchical Society: A Study of Order in World Politics*. London: Macmillan.

——. 1979. The state's positive role in world affairs. *Daedalus* 108 (4).

——. 1984. *Justice in International Relations: The Hagey Lectures*. Ontario: University of Waterloo Press.

Bull, Hedley and Adam Watson, eds. 1984. *The Expansion of International Society*. Oxford: Clarendon.

Bush, George W. 2001. *Address to a Joint Session of Congress and the American People* 20.9.01 [Available from http://www.whitehouse.gov/news/releases/2001/09/20010920-8.html].

——. 2002. *President's Remarks at the United Nations General Assembly* 12.9.02 [Available from http://www.whitehouse.gov/news/releases/2002/09/20020912-1.html].

Buzan, Barry. 2002. Who may we bomb? In *Worlds in Collision: Terror and the Future of Global Order*, edited by T. Dunne and K. Booth. Basingstoke: Palgrave.

——. 2004. *From International to World Society? English School Theory and the Social Structure of Globalisation*. Cambridge: Cambridge University Press.

Campbell, David. 1992. *Writing Security: United States Foreign Policy and the Politics of Identity*. Manchester: Manchester University Press.

——. 1998. *National Deconstruction: Violence, Identity and Justice in Bosnia*. Minneapolis: University of Minnesota Press.

Canovan, Margaret. 1974. *The Political Thought of Hannah Arendt*. London: J. M. Dent.

——. 1988. Friendship, truth and politics: Hannah Arendt and toleration. In *Justifying Toleration*, edited by S. Mendus. Cambridge: Cambridge University Press.

——. 1992. *Hannah Arendt: A Reinterpretation of her Political Thought*. Cambridge: Cambridge University Press.

——. 1996. Hannah Arendt as a conservative thinker. In *Hannah Arendt: Twenty Years later*, edited by L. May and J. Kohn. Cambridge, MA: MIT Press.

Castells, Manuel. 1996. *The Information Age: Economy, Society and Culture*. Oxford: Blackwell.

Chen, Selina. 1998. John Locke's political arguments for toleration. *History of Political Thought* 19 (2).

Cochran, Molly. 2000. *Normative Theory in International Relations: A Pragmatic Approach*. Cambridge: Cambridge University Press.

Cook, Robin. 1997. *Human Rights into a New Century*, speech delivered 17.7.97 [Available from http://www.fco.gov.uk/servlet/Front?pagename=Open Market/Xcelerate/ShowPage&c=Page&cid=1007029391647&a=KArticle&aid=1013618392902].

Copeland, Dale C. 2003. A realist critique of the English school. *Review of International Studies* 29 (3).

Cotter, Bridget. 2005. Hannah Arendt and the right to have rights. In *Hannah Arendt and International Relations: Readings Across the Lines*, edited by A. F. Lang, Jr and J. Williams. New York: Palgrave.

Cushman, Thomas and Stjepan G. Mestrovic, eds 1996. *The Time We Knew: Western Responses to Genocide in Bosnia*. New York: New York University Press.

Dallaire, Romeo. 1998. The end of innocence: Rwanda 1994. In *Hard Choices: Moral Dilemmas in Humanitarian Intervention*, edited by J. Moore. Oxford: Rowman and Littlefield.

Dershowitz, Alan M. 2002. The case for torture warrants [Available at http://www.law.harvard.edu/faculty/dershowitz/Articles/torturewarrants.html].

Diez, Thomas, ed. 2002. *The European Union and the Cyprus Conflict.* Manchester: Manchester University Press.

Dittgen, Herbert. 2000. The end of the nation-state? In *Borderlands Under Stress*, edited by M. Pratt and J. A. Brown. London: Kluwer Law International.

Dodds, Klaus. 2001. Political geography III: Critical geopolitics after ten years. *Progress in Human Geography* 25 (3).

Donnan, Hastings, and Thomas M. Wilson. 1999. *Borders: Frontiers of Identity, Nation and State.* Oxford: Berg.

Dower, Nigel. 1998. *World Ethics: The New Agenda.* Edinburgh: Edinburgh University Press.

——. 2002. Global ethics and global citizenship. In *Global Citizenship: A Critical Reader*, edited by N. Dower and J. Williams. Edinburgh: Edinburgh University Press.

Dower, Nigel and John Williams, eds 2002. *Global Citizenship: A Critical Reader.* Edinburgh: Edinburgh University Press.

——. 2002. Introduction. In *Global Citizenship: A Critical Reader*, edited by N. Dower and J. Williams. Edinburgh: Edinburgh University Press.

Dunne, Tim. 1995. The social construction of international society. *European Journal of International Relations* 1 (3).

Dunne, Tim and Nicholas J. Wheeler. 1996. Hedley Bull's pluralism of the intellect and solidarism of the will. *International Affairs* 72 (1).

Elshtain, Jean Bethke. 2004. *Just War Against Terror: The Burden of American Power in a Violent World.* New York: Basic Books.

Enloe, Cynthia. 1989. *Bananas, Beaches and Bases: Making Feminist Sense of International Relations.* London: Pandora Press.

Eyal, Jonathan. 1993. *Europe and Yugoslavia: Lessons from a Failure.* London: Royal United Services Institute.

Falk, Richard. 2002. An emergent matrix of citizenship: Complex, uneven and fluid. In *Global Citizenship: A Critical Reader*, edited by N. Dower and J. Williams. Edinburgh: Edinburgh University Press.

Finnemore, Martha and Kathryn Sikkink. 1998. International norm dynamics and political change. *International Organization* 52 (4).

Frost, Mervyn. 1996. *Ethics in International Relations.* Cambridge: Cambridge University Press.

George, Jim. 1994. *A Critical (re)introduction to International Relations.* Boulder: Lynne Reinner.

Goldsmith, Lord. 2003. *Iraq: Resolution 1441* [Available from http://www.number-10.gov.uk/output/Page7445.asp].

Gow, James. 1997. *Triumph of the Lack of Will: International Diplomacy and the Yugoslav War.* London: Hurst.

——. 2003. *The Serbian War Project and its Adversaries: A Strategy of War Crimes.* London: Hurst.

Gray, Colin S. 1999. The future is the past – with GPS. *Review of International Studies* 25 (Special issue).

——. 2002. World politics as usual after September 11: Realism vindicated. In *Worlds in Collision: Terror and the Future of Global Order*, edited by T. Dunne and K. Booth. Basingstoke: Palgrave.

Hakli, Jouni. 2001. In the territory of knowledge: State-centred discourses and the construction of society. *Progress in Human Geography* 25 (3).

Hansen, Philip. 1993. *Hannah Arendt: Politics, History and Citizenship*. Cambridge: Polity.

Harbour, Frances V. 1995. Basic moral values: A shared core. *Ethics and International Affairs* 9.

Haslam, Jonathan. 2002. *No Virtue Like Necessity: Realist Thought in International Relations Since Machiavelli*. New Haven, CT: Yale University Press.

Heater, Derek. 1996. *World Citizenship and Government: Cosmopolitan Ideas in the History of Western Political Thought*. Basingstoke: Macmillan.

Held, David. 1995. *Democracy and the Global Order: From the Modern State to Cosmopolitan Governance*. Cambridge: Polity.

Hinsley, F. H. 1963. *Power and the Pursuit of Peace: Theory and Practice in the History of Relations Between States*. Cambridge: Cambridge University Press.

Hirst, Paul and Graeme Thompson. 1999. *Globalization in Question: The International Economy and the Possibilities of Globalization*. Cambridge: Polity.

Holsti, Kalevi J. 1991. *Peace and War: Armed Conflicts and International Order, 1648–1989*. Cambridge: Cambridge University Press.

Horton, John and Susan Mendus, eds 1991. *John Locke, 'a Letter Concerning Toleration': in Focus*. London: Routledge.

Huntington, Samuel P. 1996. *The Clash of Civilizations and the Re-making of World Order*. New York: Simon and Schuster.

Hurrell, Andrew. 2002. 'There are no rules' (George W. Bush): International order after September 11. *International Relations* 16 (2).

——. 2003. International law and the making and unmaking of boundaries. In *States, Nations and Borders: The Ethics of Making Boundaries*, edited by A. Buchanan and M. Moore. Cambridge: Cambridge University Press.

Hutchings, Kimberley. 1999. *International Political Theory: Rethinking Ethics in a Global Era*. London: Sage.

Ignatieff, Michael. 2004. *The Lesser Evil: Political Ethics in an Age of Terrorism*. Edinburgh: Edinburgh University Press.

International Commission on Intervention and State Sovereignty. 2001. Responsibility to Protect. Ottawa: International Development Research Centre.

Jackson, Robert H. 2000. *The Global Covenant: Human Conduct in a World of States*. Oxford: Oxford University Press.

Jahn, Beate. 1998. Two steps forward one step back: Critical theory as the latest manifestation of liberal internationalism. *Millennium* 27 (3).

——. 2000. *The Cultural Construction of International Relations: The Invention of the State of Nature*. Basingstoke: Palgrave.

Johnson, James Turner. 2001. *Morality and Contemporary Warfare*. New Haven, CT: Yale University Press.

Jones, Bruce D. 1995. Intervention without borders: Humanitarian intervention in Rwanda. *Millennium* 24 (2).

Jones, Peter. 2001. Human rights and diverse cultures: Continuity or discontinuity? In *Human Rights and Global Diversity*, edited by S. Caney and
P. Jones. London: Frank Cass.

Kaldor, Mary. 2003. *Global Civil Society: An Answer to War*. Cambridge: Polity.

Kampfner, John. 2003. *Blair's Wars*. London: Free Press.

Kant, Immanuel. 1970 [1795]. Perpetual peace. In *Kant's Political Writings*,
edited by H. Reiss. Cambridge: Cambridge University Press.

Kedleston, Lord Curzon of. 1907. *Romanes Lecture on the Subject of Frontiers*
[Available from http://www-ibru.dur.ac.uk/docs/curzon.pdf].

Keene, Edward. 2002. *Beyond the Anarchical Society: Grotius, Colonialism and
Order in World Politics*. Cambridge: Cambridge University Press.

Keohane, Robert O. 1988. International institutions: Two approaches. *International Studies Quarterly* 32 (4).

Klein, Menachem. 2005. New and old walls in Jerusalem. *Political Geography*
24 (1).

Klusmeyer, Douglas. 2005. Hannah Arendt's Critical *Realism*: Power, justice
and responsibility. In *Hannah Arendt and International Relations: Readings
Across the Lines*, edited by A. F. Lang, Jr and J. Williams. New York:
Palgrave.

Klusmeyer, Douglas and Astri Suhrke. 2002. Comprehending 'evil': Challenges
for Law and Policy. *Ethics and International Affairs* 16 (1).

Krasner, Stephen D. 1999. *Sovereignty   Organized Hypocrisy*. Princeton, NJ:
Princeton University Press.

Kratochwil, Friedrich. 1989. *Rules, Norms and Decisions: On the Conditions of
Practical and Legal Reasoning in International Relations and Domestic Affairs*.
Cambridge: Cambridge University Press.

Lake, David A. 2003. The new sovereignty in international relations. *International Studies Review* 5 (3).

Lang, Anthony F., Jr 2002. *Agency and Ethics: The Politics of Military Intervention*.
Albany, NY: SUNY Press.

——. 2005. Governance and political action: Hannah Arendt on global political protest. In *Hannah Arendt and International Relations: Readings Across the
Lines*, edited by A. F. Lang, Jr and J. Williams. New York: Palgrave.

Lang, Anthony F., Jr and John Williams, eds 2005. *Hannah Arendt and International Relations: Readings Across the Lines*. New York: Palgrave.

Linklater, Andrew. 1990. *Beyond Realism and Marxism: Critical Theory and
International Relations*. Basingstoke: Macmillan.

——. 1998. *The Transformation of Political Community: Ethical Foundations for a
Post-Westphalian era*. Cambridge: Polity.

Little, Richard. 2000. The English school's contribution to the study of international relations. *European Journal of International Relations* 6 (3).

Lorberbaum, Menachem. 2003. Making and unmaking the boundaries of
holy land. In *States, Nations and Borders: The Ethics of Making Boundaries*,
edited by A. Buchanan and M. Moore. Cambridge: Cambridge University
Press.

Marshall, T. H. 1973. *Class, Citizenship and Social Development*. Westport, CN:
Greenwood Press.

Mayall, James. 1990. *Nationalism and International Society*. Cambridge: Cambridge University Press.

——. 2000. *World Politics: Progress and Its Limits*. Cambridge: Polity.

Mearsheimer, John J. 2001. *The Tragedy of Great Power Politics*. New York: W. W. Norton.

Melvern, Linda. 2000. *Rwanda: A Nation Betrayed*. London: Zed Press.

Mendus, Susan. 1989. *Toleration and the Limits of Liberalism*. Basingstoke: Macmillan.

Miller, David. 1995. *On Nationality*. Oxford: Clarendon.

Nadelman, Ethan A. 1990. Global prohibition regimes: The evolution of norms in international society. *International Organization* 44 (4).

Nagel, C. R. 2002. Geopolitics by another name: Immigration and the politics of assimilation. *Political Geography* 21 (8).

Newman, David. 2000. Boundaries, territory and postmodernity: Towards shared or separate spaces? In *Borderlands Under Stress*, edited by M. Pratt and J. A. Brown. London: Kluwer Law International.

——. 2004. Conflict at the interface: The impact of boundaries and borders in contemporary ethno-national conflict. In *The Geography of War and Peace*, edited by C. Flint. Oxford: Oxford University Press.

Newman, David and Anssi Paasi. 1998. Fences and neighbours in the post-modern world: Boundary narratives in political geography. *Progress in Human Geography* 22 (2).

Nussbaum, Martha. 1996. Cosmopolitanism and patriotism. In *For Love of Country: Debating the Limits of Patriotism*, edited by J. Cohen. Boston, MA: Beacon Books.

Ohmae, Kenichi. 1991. *The Borderless World: Power and Strategy in the Inter-linked Economy*. London: Fontana.

——. 1995. *The End of the Nation State: The Rise of Regional Economies*. London: HarperCollins.

——. 2001. *The Invisible Continent*. London: Nicholas Brealey.

Onuf, Nicholas Greenwood. 1989. *World of Our Making: Rules and Rule in Social Theory and International Relations*. Columbia, SC: University of South Carolina Press.

Osiander, Andreas. 2001. Sovereignty, international relations and the Westphalian myth. *International Organization* 55 (2).

Owens, Patricia. 2003. Accidents don't just happen: The liberal politics of 'high-tech' humanitarian war. *Millennium* 32 (4).

——. 2005. Hannah Arendt, violence and the inescapable fact of humanity. In *Hannah Arendt and International Relations: Readings Across the Lines*, edited by A. F. Lang, Jr and J. Williams. New York: Palgrave.

Parekh, Bhikhu. 1981. *Hannah Arendt and the Search for a New Political Philosophy*. London: Macmillan.

——. 1999. Non-ethnocentric universalism. In *Human Rights in Global Politics*, edited by T. Dunne and N. J. Wheeler. Cambridge: Cambridge University Press.

Paterson, Matthew. 2005. Green politics. In *Theories of International Relations*, edited by Scott Burchill *et al*. Basingstoke: Palgrave.

Ralph, Jason. 2005. International society, the International Criminal Court and American foreign policy. *Review of International Studies* 31 (1).

Ramsbotham, Oliver. 1997. Humanitarian intervention 1990–95: A need to reconceptualize? *Review of International Studies* 23 (4).

Rawls, John. 1993. *Political Liberalism.* New York: Columbia University Press.

———. 1999. *A Theory of Justice.* 2 edn. Oxford: Oxford University Press.

Reus-Smit, Christian. 1999. *The Moral Purpose of the State: Culture, Social Identity and Institutional Rationality in International Relations.* Princeton, NJ: Princeton University Press.

———. 2001. Imagining society: Constructivism and the English school. *British Journal of Politics and International Relations* 4 (3).

Rosenau, James N. 1997. *Along the Domestic-Foreign Frontier: Exploring Governance in a Turbulent World.* Cambridge: Cambridge University Press.

Rosenthal, Joel H. 1991. *Righteous Realists: Political Realism, Responsible Power and American Culture in the Nuclear Age.* Baton Rouge, LA: Louisiana State University Press.

Ruggie, John Gerard. 1998. Territoriality at millennium's end. In John Gerard Ruggie, *Constructing the World Polity: Essays on International Institutionalization.* London: Routledge.

———. 1998. Political Structure and Dynamic Density. In John Gerard Ruggie, *Constructing the World Polity: Essays on International Institutionalization,* London: Routledge.

———. 1998. What makes the world hang together? Neo-utilitarianism and the social constructivist challenge. *International Organization* 52 (4).

Sahnoun, Mohammed. 1998. Mixed intervention in Somalia and the Great Lakes: Culture, neutrality and the military. In *Hard Choices: Moral Dilemmas in Humanitarian Intervention,* edited by J. Moore. Oxford: Rowman and Littlefield.

Sajoo, Amyn B. 2004. *Muslim Ethics: Emerging Vistas.* London: I. B. Tauris.

Saurette, Paul. 1996. 'I mistrust all systematizers and avoid them': Nietzsche, Arendt and the crisis of the will to order in international relations theory. *Millennium* 25 (1).

Sayer, Andrew, and Michael Sorper. 1997. Ethics unbound: For a normative turn in social theory. *Environment and Planning D: Society and Space* 15 (1).

Scholte, Jan Aart. 2005. *Globalization: A Critical Introduction.* 2 edn. Basingstoke: Palgrave.

Shapcott, Richard. 2001. *Justice, Community and Dialogue in International Relations.* Cambridge: Cambridge University Press.

———. 2004. IR as practical philosophy: Defining a 'classical approach'. *British Journal of Politics and International Relations* 6 (3).

Shapiro, Michael and Hayward Alker, eds 1996. *Challenging Boundaries: Global Flows, Territorial Identities.* Minneapolis: University of Minnesota Press.

Shaw, Martin. 2002. *Who May We Bomb: A Reply to Barry Buzan* [Available from http://www.theglobalsite.ac.uk/justpeace/111ashaw.htm].

Shue, Henry. 1996. *Basic Rights: Subsistence, Affluence and US Foreign Policy.* 2 edn. Princeton, NJ: Princeton University Press.

Sidaway, James D. 2003. Sovereign Excess? Portraying Postcolonial City-scapes. *Political Geography* 22 (2).

Singer, Peter. 1985 [1972]. Famine, affluence and morality. In *International Ethics*, edited by Charles R. Beitz, *et al.* Princeton, NJ: Princeton University Press.

Smith, Anthony D. 1991. *National Identity*. London: Penguin.

Smith, David M. 1998. How far should we care? On the spatial scope of benef-icence. *Progress in Human Geography* 22 (1).

——. 1999. Geography and ethics: How far should we go? *Progress in Human Geography* 23 (1).

——. 2001. Geography and ethics: Progress, or more of the same? *Progress in Human Geography* 25 (2).

Smith, Steve. 2000. International relations: Still an American social science? *British Journal of Politics and International Relations* 2 (3).

Smith, Steve, Ken Booth, and Marysia Zalewski, eds 1996. *International Theory: Positivism and Beyond*. Cambridge: Cambridge University Press.

Spruyt, Hendrik. 1994. *The Sovereign State and its Competitors: An Analysis of Systems Change*. Princeton, NJ: Princeton University Press.

Starr, Harvey and G. Dale Thomas. 2005. The nature of borders and interna-tional conflict: Revisiting hypotheses on territory. *International Studies Quarterly* 49 (1).

Statman, Daniel. 2003. Man-made boundaries and man-made holiness in the Jewish tradition. In *States, Nations and Borders: The Ethics of Making Bounda-ries*, edited by A. Buchanan and M. Moore. Cambridge: Cambridge Univer-sity Press.

Strange, Susan. 1998. Globaloney. *Review of International Political Economy* 5.

——. 1999. The 'westfailure' system. *Review of International Studies* 25 (3).

Straw, Jack. 2002. *Failed and Failing States*, speech delivered 6.9.02 [Available from http://www.fco.gov.uk/servlet/Front?pagename=OpenMarket/Xcelerate/ShowPage&c=Page&cid=1007029391647&a=KArticle&aid=1031273860289].

——. 2002. *Principles of a Modern Global Community*, speech delivered 10.4.02 [Available from http://www.fco.gov.uk/servlet/Front?pagename=OpenMarket/Xcelerate/ShowPage&c=Page&cid=1007029391647&a=KArticle&aid=1018466002161].

——. 2004. *We must Engage in Europe and in the Wider World*, speech delivered 21.4.04 [Available from http://www.fco.gov.uk/servlet/Front?pagename=OpenMarket/Xcelerate/ShowPage&c=Page&cid=1007029391647&a=KArticle&aid=1079980004115].

Sutch, Peter. 2000. Human rights as settled norms: Mervyn Frost and the limits of Hegelian human rights theory. *Review of International Studies* 26 (2).

Teschke, Benno. 2003. *The Myth of 1648: Class, Geopolitics and the Making of Modern International Relations*. London: Verso.

Teson, Fernando. 1998. *Humanitarian Intervention: An Enquiry into Law and Morality*. Dobbs Ferry: Transnational Publishers.

Thuathail, Gearóid Ó. 1996. *Critical Geopolitics: The Politics of Writing Global Space*. London: Routledge.

Thucydides. 1923. *History of the Peloponnesian War*. Translated by C. F. Smith. London: Loeb Classic Library.

Tickner, J. Ann. 1992. *Gender in International Relations: Feminist Perspectives on Achieving Global Security*. New York: Columbia University Press.

Tinder, Glenn. 1976. *Tolerance: Toward a New Civility*. Amherst, MA: University of Massachusetts Press.

Vasquez, John A. 1993. *The War Puzzle*. Cambridge: Cambridge University Press.

Vincent, John. 1974. *Non-intervention and International Order*. Princeton, NJ: Princeton University Press.

Walker, R. B. J. 1992. *Inside/Outside: International Relations as Political Theory*. Cambridge: Cambridge University Press.

Walt, Stephen M and John J. Mearsheimer. 2003. An unnecessary war. *Foreign Policy* (134).

Walter, Barbara F. 2003. Explaining the intractability of territorial conflict. *International Studies Review* 5 (4).

Walters, William. 2002. De-naturalising the border: The politics of Schengen-land. *Environment and Planning D: Society and Space* 20 (5).

Waltz, Kenneth. 1979. *Theory of International Politics*. New York: Addison Wesley Longman.

Walzer, Michael. 1983. *Spheres of Justice: A Defence of Pluralism and Equality*. Oxford: Robertson.

———. 1994. *Thick and Thin: Moral Argument at Home and Abroad*. London: University of Notre Dame Press.

———. 2002. *Just and Unjust Wars: A Moral Argument with Historical Illustrations*. 3 ed. New York: Basic Books.

———. 2004. *Arguing About War*. New Haven, CT: Yale University Press.

Watson, Adam. 1992. *The Evolution of International Society*. London: Routledge.

Wendt, Alexander. 1999. *Social Theory of International Politics*. Cambridge: Cambridge University Press.

Wheeler, Nicholas J. 1992. Pluralist or solidarist conceptions of international society. *Millennium* 21 (3).

———. 1996. Guardian angel or global gangster? A review of the ethical claims of international society. *Political Studies* 44 (1).

———. 1999. Humanitarian vigilantes or legal entrepreneurs? Enforcing human rights in international society. In *Human Rights and Global Diversity*, edited by S. Caney and P. Jones. London: Frank Cass.

———. 2000. *Saving Strangers: Humanitarian Intervention in International Society*. Oxford: Oxford University Press.

———. 2002. Dying for 'Enduring Freedom': accepting responsibility for civilian casualties in the war against terrorism. *International Relations* 16 (2).

Wight, Martin. 1977. *Systems of States*. Leicester: Leicester University Press.

Wight, Martin (edited by Gabrielle Wight and Brian Porter). 1991. *International Theory: The Three Traditions*. Leicester: Leicester University Press.

Williams, John. 1998. Mervyn Frost and the constitution of liberalism. *Journal of Peace Research* 35 (4).

——. 1999. The ethical basis of humanitarian intervention, the Security Council and Yugoslavia. *International Peacekeeping* 6 (2).

——. 1999. The ethics of borders and the borders of ethics: International society and rights and duties of special beneficence. *Global Society* 13 (4).

——. 2002. Territorial borders, toleration and the English school. *Review of International Studies* 28 (4).

——. 2003. Territorial borders, international ethics and political geography: Do good fences still make good neighbours? *Geopolitics* 8 (2).

——. 2005. Hannah Arendt and the international 'space in-between'. In *Hannah Arendt and International Relations: Readings Across the Lines*, edited by A. F. Lang, Jr and J. Williams. New York: Palgrave.

——. 2005. Pluralism, solidarism and the emergence of world society in English school theory. *International Relations* 19 (1).

——. 2006. Order and Society. In *The Anarchical Society in a Globalized World*, edited by R. Little and J. Williams. Basingstoke: Palgrave.

Williams, John, with Anthony F. Lang, Jr 2005. Introduction. In *Hannah Arendt and International Relations: Readings Across the Lines*, edited by A. F. Lang, Jr and J. Williams. New York: Palgrave.

Williams, John with Tim Roach. 2006. Security, territorial borders and british Iraq policy: Buying a Blair way to heaven? *Geopolitics* 11(1).

Zacher, Mark W. 2002. The territorial integrity norm: International boundaries and the use of force. *International Organization* 55 (2).

Index